400 ILLUSTRATIONS
FOR MINISTERS
AND TEACHERS

Prochnow Speaker's Library

---

400 ILLUSTRATIONS FOR MINISTERS AND TEACHERS

Herbert V. Prochnow

Baker Books
A Division of Baker Book House Co
Grand Rapids, Michigan 49516

FOREWORD

In this book, humorous, serious and inspiring stories, illustrations, epigrams, quotations and biographical sketches are mingled freely. Each item has a title. In addition, all items are indexed so that the reader can quickly locate items related to the subject on which he needs stories and illustrative material.

Moreover, almost every item can be used in a variety of ways which will occur to the reader as he browses through the wealth of material in the book.

PREFACE

This book is meant to assist ministers, Sunday school super-intendents and teachers, and all who lead classes and discussions, conduct meetings of church groups of men and women and speak in public. Leaders of all types of church, charitable and youth organizations will find this book of practical use on many occasions and an invaluable reference book.

In this volume there are more than 400 items of all kinds. Humorous and serious stories, witty epigrams, inspiring quotations from literature, and unusual illustrations from sermons and biographies are all included in this collection.

A good story will often help to make clear an important point in a class discussion. A short and interesting epigram, witticism, or quotation will frequently serve to emphasize convincingly some part of a report that needs to be stressed. An inspiring selection from a sermon or an exceptional incident from the life of a distinguished person will often convey a message that will be long remembered.

The items in the book have been carefully indexed to assist the reader promptly to find those related to his particular needs.

Here is a book containing hundreds of stories, epigrams, witticisms, quotations, selections from sermons, and incidents from biography which have been chosen to provide helpful, inspiring and stimulating material.

HERBERT V. PROCHNOW

STORIES—ILLUSTRATIONS—
QUOTATIONS

OCCASIONAL THOUGHTS

The measure of a man is not the number of servants he has, but the number of people he serves.

It is right to be contented with what you have, but never with what you are.

The secret of true greatness is simplicity.

Life is like a mirror—if you frown at it, it frowns back; if you smile, it returns the greeting.

GUEST TOWELS

We are having company. You say, how do I know? Well, a little birdie didn't tell me so.

Just came in from school, all smeared with dirt; Mom's all spic and span, her manner rather curt. "Please be careful! Don't touch that! Jimmie, *please!* Put out that cat!"

A frosted cake—Mom's special lure. Company coming? I'm not sure. Up to the bathroom—I'll find out. Yep! I thought so —there's no doubt. Dinky little towels hanging there just so; pink and white forget-me-nots folded so they'll show.

Now, that means I've got to scrub my ears and nails and such. And not a *useful* towel in sight—just the ones you *mustn't touch!*   *F. M. Scott, Three Rivers, Michigan*

BEATITUDES FOR A HOUSEWIFE

Blessed is she whose daily tasks are a labor of love, for she translates duty into privilege.

Blessed is she who mends stockings and toys and broken hearts, for her understanding is a balm to humanity.

Blessed is she who serves laughter and smiles at every meal, for she shall be blessed with goodness.

Blessed is she who preserves the sanctity of the Christian home, for here is a sacred trust that crowns her with dignity.

Cheerful News, Eagle Rock, California

ALL WHO BELIEVE THIS

Two cars met in a head-on collision. Both drivers got out and began to apologize profusely.

"I'm so sorry," said the woman. "It was my fault."

"Not at all, madam," the man responded with gallantry; "I was completely to blame."

"But I was on your side of the road," protested the woman.

"That may be true, madam," replied the man positively, "but I am responsible for the accident. I saw you coming three blocks away, and had plenty of time to have turned down a side street." *Capper's Weekly*

NEVER SATISFIED

A man who conducted a modern motel for years on a busy highway complained bitterly about the effect on his business when a new superhighway was put through nearby. Finally one of the neighbors became impatient hearing him talk about it.

"Look here, Cal," said he, "I see a *No Vacancy* sign out in front of your place every night. You should worry!"

"You can't go by that," replied Cal. "Before they put the turnpike through I used to turn away 25 or 30 people every night. Since the turnpike, I don't turn away more'n 12 or 15."

Duncannon Record in Pathfinder

EXPERIENCE

Experience is a wonderful thing. It enables you to recognize a mistake when you make it again.

OPTIMIST

An optimist is a man who, instead of feeling sorry he cannot pay his bills, is glad he is not one of his creditors.

PECULIAR

Funny, isn't it? The stupid in this world are cocksure, and the intelligent are full of doubt.

TO KEEP FROM GROWING OLD

Always race trains to crossings. Engineers like it. It breaks the monotony.

Always pass the car ahead on curves. Don't use the horn, it may unnerve other drivers.

Demand half the road—the middle half. Insist on your rights.

Always speed. It shows you're full of pep, even though you are an amateur driver.

Don't waste time stopping, looking or listening. Everybody else does that.

Always lock your brakes when skidding. It makes the job seem more artistic.

In sloppy weather drive close to pedestrians. Dry cleaners appreciate this.

Always drive with your window closed. Then you don't have to signal. *Motor News*

THE FELLOW WHO CAN TAKE IT

Does it hurt you very much to lose a contest? If it doesn't, you weren't very anxious to win, and didn't do your best. To anyone who makes an honest effort to win, it hurts to lose.

But one ought to be a good loser, and a good loser always gives the other fellow credit for what he does. Here's a thought that will help you bear your defeat, if you can remember it at the right time: *A good licking is sometimes the best thing that can happen to you.* Why?

If you would win all the time, you might soon get an exaggerated idea of your own ability and importance, and would lose your modesty and your good sense.

The chances are, the fellow who wins too often loses his sportsmanship. That is what happens to many great champions. When they finally lose, they are so disappointed that they are down and out. The fellow who loses once in a while, and can take it, usually makes a success of life. *Sunshine Magazine*

GENERAL MacARTHUR'S FATHER'S PRAYER

Build me a son, O Lord, who will be strong enough to know when he is weak and brave enough to face himself when he is afraid; one who will be proud and unbending in honest defeat, but humble and gentle in victory. Build me a son whose wishes will not replace his actions—a son who will know Thee, and that to know himself is the foundation stone of knowledge. Send him, I pray, not in the path of ease and comfort but the stress and spur of difficulties and challenge; here let him learn to stand up in the storm, here let him learn compassion for those who fail.

Build me a son whose heart will be clear, whose goal will be high; a son who will master himself before he seeks to master others; one who will learn to laugh, yet never forget how to weep; one who will reach into the future, yet never forget the past, and after all these things are his, this I pray, enough sense of humor that he may always be serious yet never take himself too seriously. Give him humility so that he may always remember the simplicity of true greatness, the open mind of true wisdom, the meekness of true strength; then I, his father, will dare to whisper, "I have not lived in vain."

RANDOM THOUGHTS

So long as there are human beings to reach for the stars, the world will move on.

You can't keep trouble from coming, but you needn't give it a chair to sit on. *Old Proverb*

If you would stand well with a great mind, leave him with a favorable impression of yourself; if with a little mind, leave him with a favorable impression of himself.

A cure for covetousness: Think of something to give instead of something to get.

We work better when we work from love, not merely doing our duty in an indifferent way.

We wrong others by unjust thoughts as well as by unkind speech and unfair deeds. Thought is not powerless; it creates an atmosphere that hinders or helps.

No person was ever honored for what he received. Honor has been the reward for what he gave. *Coolidge*

I am an old man and have known a great many troubles, but most of them never happened. *Mark Twain*

THE UNCOMMON MAN

Among the delusions offered us by fuzzy-minded people is that imaginary creature, the common man. It is dinned into us that this is the century of the common man. The whole idea is another cousin of the Soviet Proletariat. The uncommon man is to be whittled down to size. It is the negation of individual dignity and a slogan of mediocrity.

The common man dogma may be of use as a vote-getting apparatus. It supposedly proves the humility of demagogues.

The greatest strides of human progress have come from uncommon men and women. You have perhaps heard of George Washington, Abraham Lincoln, or Thomas Edison. They were humble in origin, but that was not their greatness.

The humor of it is that, when we get sick, we want an uncommon doctor. When we go to war we yearn for an uncommon general or admiral. When we choose the president of a university, we want an uncommon educator.

The imperative need of this nation at all times is the leadership of the uncommon men or women. We need men and women who cannot be intimidated, who are not concerned with applause meters, nor those who sell tomorrow for cheers today.

Such leaders are not to be made like queen bees. America recognizes no frozen social stratifications which prevent the free rise of every individual. They must rise by their own merits.   *Herbert Hoover*

YOU CAN MAKE YOURSELF MIND YOU

"How did you keep from crying?" someone asked a little girl who had fallen down and hurt her knee. "Oh," she answered, "I just said to myself, 'Stop that,' and made myself mind me."

NO RAIN

A visitor to New Mexico was talking to a sun-browned native, and commented on the lack of rain. "Doesn't it ever rain here?" the tourist asked.

The native thought a moment and said, "Mister, do you remember the story of Noah and the Ark, and how it rained 40 days and 40 nights?"

"Sure I do," said the tourist.

"Well," drawled the native, "we got a half-inch that time."

FAR SIGHTED

Old gentleman: "You're an honest boy, but it was a $10 bill, not ten ones, that I lost."

Honest Boy: "I know, Mister, it was a $10 bill I picked up. But the last time I found one, the man who owned it didn't have any change."

FRIENDS

Two enemies are just two potential friends who don't know each other.

THE DIFFERENCE

Little Tommy was asked the difference between prose and poetry. He pondered awhile, and then said, "There was a young man named Reeze, who went into a pond to his ankle. That's prose, but if the water had been a few inches higher, it would have been poetry."

TWO GOLDEN DAYS

There are two days of the week upon which and about which I never worry. Two carefree days kept sacredly free from fear and apprehension. One of these days is yesterday; with all its pains and aches, all its faults and blunders, it has passed forever beyond the reach of my recall. Save for the beautiful memories, sweet and tender, that linger like the perfume of roses in the heart of the day that has gone, I have nothing to do with yesterday. It was mine; it is God's.

And the other day I do not worry about is tomorrow, with all its possibilities, adversities, its burdens, its perils, its large promise. Its sun will rise in roseate splendor, or behind a mask of clouds. But it will rise. Tomorrow—it will be mine.

There is left for myself, then, but one day of the week—

today. Any man can fight the battles of today. Any woman can carry the burdens of just one day.

Therefore, I think, and I do, and I journey for but one day at a time. And while faithfully and dutifully I run my course, and work my appointed task on this one day, God the Almighty takes care of yesterday and tomorrow.   *Robert J. Burdett*

LIFE'S RESPONSIBILITIES

If we work upon marble, it will perish. If we work upon brass, time will efface it. If we rear temples, they will crumble to dust. But if we work upon men's immortal minds, if we imbue them with high principles, with the just fear of God and love of their fellow men, we engrave on those tablets something which no time can efface, and which will brighten and brighten to all eternity.   *Daniel Webster, Speech, Faneuil Hall, 1852*

What makes the world go round is the courage to attempt something that can't be done and to succeed.

Man must cease attributing his problems to his environment, and learn again to exercise his will—his personal responsibility in the realm of faith and morals.   *Albert Schweitzer*

A SUMMER CREED

I believe in the flowers, and their glorious indifference to the changes of the morrow.

I believe in the birds, and their implicit trust in the loving Providence that feeds them.

I believe in the prayer-chanting brooks, as they murmur a sweet hope of finding the far distant sea to which they patiently run.

I believe in the whispering winds, for they teach me to listen to the still small voice within my feverish soul.

I believe in the vagrant clouds, as they remind me that life, like a summer day, must have some darkness to reveal its hidden meaning.

I believe in the soft-speaking rains, accented with warm tears, telling me that nothing will grow save it be fertilized with tears.

I believe in the golden hush of the sunsets, reflecting a momentary glory of that world beyond my little horizon.

I believe in the soft-falling dew, revealing the infinite spring of living waters for things parched and withered.

I believe in the holiness of twilight, as it gives me a sense of the presence of God, and I know that I am not alone. And whatever else I believe is enshrined in those abiding feelings that lie too deep for words.

W. Waldemar W. Argow in Scottish Rite News Bulletin

WHEN LIFE BEGINS

For some life may begin at 40. For others, life begins when they first begin to think of themselves last.

RESPONSIBILITY

No one is responsible for all the things that happen to him, but he is responsible for the way he acts when they do happen.

THOUGHTS

All mankind is divided into three classes: those that are immovable, those that are movable, and those that move.

Benjamin Franklin

Goodness consists not in the outward things we do, but in the inward things we are.   *E. H. Chapin*

We see things not as they are, but as *we* are.

H. M. Tomlinson

A thankful heart is the parent of all virtues.

Marcus Cicero, Roman orator

FAITH

No ray of sunlight is ever lost, but the green which it wakes into existence needs time to sprout, and it is not always granted to the sower to live to see the harvest. All work that is worth anything is done in faith. *Albert Schweitzer*

POINT OF VIEW

An Englishman moved to the United States after the end of World War II, and immediately took out his American citizenship papers. Several months later he was visited in this country by an English relative who sternly reprimanded him for becoming an American citizen.

"What have you to gain by becoming an American?" he asked.

"Well," replied the other, "for one thing I won the American Revolution."

WHEN YOU SHARE

Those who raise flowers find that if they pick them the plants continue to bear flowers all summer; if they do not allow them to be touched, they go to seed and wither and die. Flowers are not the only pleasures that are doubled or trebled if they are shared. Many of the greatest joys of life shrivel away if we try jealously to keep every bit for ourselves.

SOMETHING HEAVY

Little Harry came running into the house crying. The top of his head showed a bad bruise.

"What fell on your head?" asked his little sister.

"I did," sobbed Harry.

SANCTUARY

I like to go into a place
When only God is there,
And bending low upon my knees
I bow my head in prayer.
No doubt or fear can touch me there,
My spirit is at rest,
For I am in my Father's house,
A loved and sheltered guest.
And when I must go forth again
Where men indifferent plod,
I am the better for the time
That I have spent with God!   *From Sanskrit*

A SON

During World War II, Brig. Gen. Theodore Roosevelt, Jr., was waiting at an airport for a plane. A sailor stepped to a ticket window and asked for a seat on the same plane, explaining, "I want to see my mother; I ain't got much time."

The indifferent young thing at the ticket window was not impressed. "There's a war on, you know," she exclaimed.

At this point Gen. Roosevelt stepped to the window and told her to give the sailor his seat. A friend spoke his surprise. "Teddy, aren't you in a hurry, too?"

"It's a matter of rank," came the reply. "I'm only a general; he's a son!"   *James Keller in One Moment, Please*

MY HOUSE

I am the sole owner of a house I have lived in over eighty-seven years. In the beginning it was a splendid structure, large enough, tall enough, and on a solid foundation. It was an attractive house. I was proud of its appearance.

I have never paid much attention to the repairs on the outside; only to keep it fresh and healthy looking. But I have striven to make the interior sweet and clean and beautiful. No unwelcome guests, such as anger, jealousy, and unkindness, were allowed to linger long within its sacred walls, but rather such lovely ones as love, sympathy, prayer, and goodwill every day. So it has been a joy to dwell in this house of mine.

But time is proving that all things, however beautiful, must fade, and so my house is going down. The windows are not so clear, the door is a bit squeaky, the roof is near to cracking, and the foundation is getting trembly. And I know that some day, not far off, I must move out and let this old house crumble into dust. But the tenant within is quiet, patient; living on the food of the promises of the Good Book, to guide to the House not made with hands.

So I say to this old house of mine, as we have grown old together: "Oh! House, we have been long together, in pleasant and in cloudy weather. . . . Choose thine own time; say not 'Good Night,' but in some brighter clime, bid me 'Good Morning.' "   *By Mother Conger in Sunshine Magazine*

VERY FEW

Remarked the wife, "Everyone in town is talking about the Smiths' quarrel. Some are taking his part, and some are taking hers."

"And," interrupted her husband, "I suppose a few eccentric individuals are minding their own business."

HE KNEW

"I guess I'll be staying up late tonight," little Billy told a couple of his pals. "I promised Dad I'd help him with my homework."

RANDOM THOUGHTS

The greatest wealth is to live content with little; for there is never want where the mind is satisfied.   *Lucretius*

True Christian charity is not just giving a man a dime when he is hungry. It is giving a man a dime when you are as hungry as he is and need the dime just as badly.

You must not lose faith in humanity. Humanity is an ocean; if a few drops of the ocean are dirty, the ocean does not become dirty.   *Mahatma Gandhi*

It is not enough for the gardener to love flowers; he must also hate weeds.

JOHN THREE SIXTEEN

For God—the Lord of earth and heaven,
So loved—and longed to see forgiven,
The world—in sin and pleasure mad,
That He gave—the greatest gift He had—
His only begotten Son—to take our place;
That whosoever—Oh, what grace!
Believeth—placing simple trust
In Him—the righteous and the just,
Should not perish—lost in sin,
But have eternal life—in Him.   *Sunshine Magazine*

SAVED TEN DOLLARS

Once, when John Garner was Vice President of the United States, his enthusiasm for the local baseball team caused him to lose a $10 bet.

"Will you autograph the bill, Mr. Garner?" the winner requested. "I'm giving it to my son as a memento. He will want to frame it and hang it in his room."

"You mean he won't spend it?" asked Garner.

"Indeed not!"

"In that case," said Garner, I'll just write you a check."

A SUBSTITUTE

A minister was called upon to substitute for the regular minister, who had failed to reach the church because he was delayed in a snowstorm. The speaker began by explaining the meaning of a substitute. "If you break a window," he said, "and then place a cardboard there instead, that is a substitute."

After the sermon, a woman, who had listened intently, shook hands with him, and wishing to compliment him, said, "You were no substitute—you were a real pane!"

Capper's Weekly

LIFE

No one is useless in the world who lightens the burden of it for anyone else.   *Charles Dickens*

By accepting good advice, you are increasing your own ability.

A good name, like good will, is attained by many actions, and may be lost by one.

Those at the top have reached their positions by tackling uphill jobs.

Worry often gives a small thing a big shadow.

Swedish Proverb

SPEAKING AT LENGTH

The sermon went on and on and on in the heat of the church. At last the minister paused and asked:

"What more, my friends, can I say?"

In the back of the church a voice whispered to a neighbor: "Amen."

THAT'S DIFFERENT

"Well, Jack, how does it feel to be a grandfather?"

"Oh, it's good news, of course, but I'll have to get used to the idea of being married to a grandmother!"

WHAT TO DO?

A little boy came home from school and announced to his mother: "I'm in a fine fix at school. The teacher says I have to write more legibly, and if I do, she'll find out that I can't spell!"

SLOW ME DOWN

Slow me down, Lawd. Ah's goin' too fast. An cain't see mah bruther when he's walking past. Ah miss a lot o' good things day by day; Ah doan't know a blessin' when it comes mah way. Slow me down, Lawd. Ah wants t' see more o' th' things that's good fur me. A little less o' me an' a mite more o' you; Ah wants th' heavenly atmosphere t' trickle through. Let me help a bruther when th' goin's rough; when folks work t'gether it ain't so tough. Slow me down, Lawd, so I c'n talk with some o' your angels; slow me down t' a walk.

"Capricorn" in Chicago Tribune

HE ALSO GOT A DRUM

A friend reports that a few evenings ago, in a traffic snarl, one of the inevitable horn-tooters began blasting his horn almost continuously. A man in a car alongside looked over and politely inquired, "What else did you get for Christmas?"

THINGS YOU NEVER REGRET

Showing kindness to an aged person. Destroying the letter written in anger. Offering the apology that saves a friendship. Stopping a scandal that is wrecking a reputation. Helping a boy find himself. Taking time to show consideration to your parents. Remembering God in all things.   *The Echo*

SOME OLD VIRTUES

The practical thing we can do, if we really want to make the world over again, says ex-President Herbert Hoover, is to try out the word "old" for awhile. There are some old things that make this country. There is the old virtue of religious faith. There are the old virtues of integrity and the whole truth. There is the old virtue of incorruptible service and honor in public office. There are the old virtues of economy in government, of self-reliance, thrift, and individual liberty. There are the old virtues of patriotism, real love of country, and willingness to sacrifice for it.

BE STILL!

Every great song, story, painting, sculpture, invention or humanitarian work has come out of the "still place." The creators of the world's work and men of genius know how to be still. In that stillness a new idea comes to mind, and they work to bring it into visible form.

Thomas Edison lived and worked in the "still place" twenty hours out of the twenty-four. He slept little and talked seldom. He said he was glad to be deaf, for he did not have to listen to the chatter of people. He took no credit to himself for his electrical inventions and discoveries. "Had I not been there to get it," he said, "someone else would." He knew he was just an instrument for divine power and wisdom to work through, but he kept the dial of his mind tuned to the universal station.

George Washington Carver contacted that same creative power that is always ready and waiting to be used. It was a rule of this great scientist to rise at 4:00 A.M., and go out into the woods or fields. In the stillness of the dawn he asked what he was to do that day, and waited for God to tell him. He took the humble peanut to his laboratory and reverently asked God what a peanut was and why He made it, and it yielded more than three hundred products to his scientific experiments. The sweet potato gave him two hundred more useful products and increased its yield 500 per cent. Agricultural living of the South was transformed by this great Negro working so humbly with God in the "still place." Asking nothing for himself, he brought unnumbered blessings not only to his own race, but to the Southland.   *Mabel Powers in Boy Life*

EPIGRAMS

Gossip: Something that goes in one ear and out the mouth.

An argument is where two people are trying to get in the last word first.

When you feel dog-tired at night, it may be because you've growled all day long.

It is difficult to save money when your neighbors keep buying things you can't afford.

WAYS TO KILL A CHURCH

Looking through an old notebook, I came upon a message received twenty-five years ago by an eminent clergyman, Dr. Robert Freeman. It was entitled, "Fourteen Ways to Kill a Church." According to that document, here are the rules for killing a church:

1. Don't come.
2. If you do come, come late.
3. When you come, come with a grouch.
4. At every service ask yourself, "What do I get out of this?"
5. Never accept office. It is better to stay outside and criticize.
6. Visit other churches about half the time to let your minister know you are not tied to him. There is nothing like independence.

7. Let the pastor earn his money; let him do all the work.
8. Sit pretty well back and never sing. If you do sing, sing out of tune and behind everybody else.
9. Never pay in advance. Wait until you get your money's worth, and then wait a bit longer.
10. Never encourage the preacher. If you like a sermon keep mum about it. Many a preacher has been ruined by flattery. Don't let his blood be on your head!
11. It is good to tell your pastor's failings to any strangers that might happen in. They might be a long time finding them out.
12. Of course, you can't be expected to get new members for the church with such a pastor.
13. If your church unfortunately happens to be harmonious, call it apathy, or indifference or lack of zeal, or anything under the sun except what it is.
14. If there happen to be a few zealous workers in the church, make a tremendous protest against the church being run by a clique.

Such negative attitudes, in the spirit of criticism, unwillingness to work together, chronic unfriendliness, failure at cooperation would kill a church, or any other institution. Thank God that is not the spirit of our churches today. Today we can list fourteeen counterpoints on "How to Have a Living Church":

1. Always attend.
2. Always come well ahead of starting time.
3. Come with a holy glow, a radiant countenance, a happy mood.
4. Come expectantly, expecting to offer yourself to God in service.
5. Accept office when called thereto and serve faithfully the decisions of the officers, even though they may not always be your personal judgments.
6. When you visit other churches, observe helpful suggestions for your own church. So treasure your own church

that to be absent from its service of worship is a minus factor in any week.

7. So do the work of a good layman that the pastor need not do all the work but is free to do the work of a faithful pastor.
8. Sit up as near the front as may be possible and sing out on all the hymns.
9. Always tithe, pledge in advance, pay in advance, and —if you are to be absent—remember that the church's expenses will continue.
10. Always encourage your pastor. He will have enough discouragements from other sources.
11. Speak up for the fine things about your church; the weak points are conspicuous enough.
12. Win all the people you can to Christ and the Church, no matter who your pastor is. You are committing them to Christ and the Church and not to your pastor.
13. Always contribute to the peace, purity, and unity of the church.
14. Rejoice that no clique operates a living church. Rejoice that the fellowship of believers is not a patrician communion but a people's church in which there can be no functional clique or monopoly by a few.

How wonderful it is that in this age it is the latter fourteen rules which are being lived out rather than the former negative ones. *From a sermon by Dr. Edward L. R. Elson of The National Presbyterian Church, Washington, D. C.*

HEADS BENT LOW

A stooped old man and a brisk young man chanced to meet one day. The young man said to the older one, in his usual braggart way:

"Why don't you walk up straight like me? That's no way to grow old. It's all a form of habit—at least that's what I'm told."

The old man gave him a knowing look, and said:

"My dear young friend, have you ever examined a fine wheat

field, and noticed the heads that bend? If not, just look them over close, as the harvest time draws nigh. You'll find the heads that are quite empty are standing tall and high, but the heads that count in the harvest time are filled, and bending low, awaiting the reaper's bright sickle—their time is short, you know."

And as the young man passed on by, he slowly bowed his head. No doubt he pondered many a day on the things the old man said. *From an Old England source*

ONE DAY

Anyone can carry his burden, however hard, until nightfall. Anyone can do his work, however hard, one day. Anyone can live sweetly, patiently, lovingly, purely, till the sun goes down. And this is all that life really means. *Robert Louis Stevenson*

MOTHER

Mother, having finally tucked a small boy into bed after an unusually trying day: "Well, I've worked today from son-up to son-down!"

A FUTURE MATHEMATICIAN

Little boy Billy went into a candy store and asked, "How much are your candy sticks?"

The clerk answered, "Six for five cents."

Bill thought and said, "Six for five cents, five for four cents, four for three cents, three for two cents, two for one cent, and one for nothing. I'll take one, please."

IS THAT NICE?

A small boy was bored on a long trip. Suddenly he turned to his father and said, "I wish you'd let Mother drive—it's more exciting!"

LIKE BANANAS

Last Spring a recent bride was showing a friend her garden, the first she had ever planted. The friend noticed several small green clusters at one end of the plot, and asked what they were. "Radishes," said the bride.

"How interesting," commented the friend. "Most gardeners plant them in rows."

"They do?" puzzled the bride. "That seems strange. They always come in bunches at the store."

NOT TOO FAST

Two women were preparing to board the airliner. One of them turned to the pilot and said, "Now, please don't travel faster than sound. We want to talk."

WHAT DO YOU REALLY TRY TO DO?

When you seek to know what a man's ideal of life is, do not ask, "What does the man say?" His words may mislead you as his posings deceive him. Inquire only, "What does this man really try to do?" When we find out what a man who can choose his lines of life steadily strives to do, we have found out what he really wishes to be; we know what his ideal is.

Sunshine Magazine

WORTH REMEMBERING

A boy who does his best today will be a hard man to beat tomorrow.

OPPORTUNITY TRIED TO KNOCK

There is a familiar proverb to the effect that "Opportunity knocks on every man's door once, but only once." Here are a few instances when her knock was not heard:

It is difficult to give proper recognition to those who loaned Robert Fulton the money for his steamboat project. So fearful of ridicule were his backers that they stipulated that their names be withheld!

When George Westinghouse had perfected his airbrake, in 1875, he offered it to Commodore Vanderbilt. The railroad magnate returned Westinghouse's letter, with these words scribbled across the bottom. "I have no time to waste on fools."

One day a stranger approached Mark Twain with a request for $500, for which he would sell half interest in his invention. Twain, "bit" several times before, refused flatly. But out of courtesy he asked the stranger his name. "Bell," the man replied, as he turned away, "Alexander Graham Bell."

Webb B. Garrison in THE UPLIFT

COULDN'T FOOL HIM

It looked as if both the hero and the heroine of the Western movie were doomed. They were surrounded completely by redmen.

One of the little boys in the front row sniffed, "If he had kept his eye on the Indians instead of the girl, this never would have happened."

ALWAYS INNOCENT

A young woman was returning from a shopping tour when she encountered a traffic officer writing out a ticket for overtime parking. Quite angry when her dissuasive tactics were of no avail, she snapped, "Young fellow, what procedure do you use when you catch someone who really is guilty?"

"I don't know, ma'am," the officer replied respectfully, as he handed her the ticket. "All I ever catch are the innocent ones."

BLESS THIS CHURCH

Bless this church, which towers so high,
Reaching tall through God's blue sky,
Bless the door we enter through,
Bringing us so near to you.
Bless the Bible, given by you,
Showing us what we should do;
Bless each page that lies therein,
Leading us away from sin.

Bless the altar standing there,
Represented by a prayer.
Help us all on bended knee
To be united, one in Thee.
Bless the windows' colored hue,
Bringing sunshine straight from you.
Bless the minister, that he
May be ever close to Thee.

Bless this world, and may it be
At lasting peace, O Lord, with Thee.

Mary Ruth Crawford

A CHINESE PROVERB

If there is righteousness in the heart, there will be beauty in character. If there is beauty in character, there will be harmony·in the home. If there is harmony in the home, there will be order in the nation. If there is order in the nation, there will be peace in the world.

SEVEN DEADLY SINS

Politics without principle; wealth without work; pleasure without character; business without morality; science without humanity; and worship without sacrifice.   *E. Stanley Jones*

WHAT OUR FOREFATHERS LEFT US

A nation under God—what a tradition that is. It involves much: our way of life, our social and political morals, the wise use of our freedom, our common decencies. Those who came first to the eastern shores of our country did not seek gold at the end of their rainbow. They sought better things than that. They sought a drama of spiritual adventure. They sought a new way of life. They found the will to carve out of the forest a nation under God. To this purpose men held fast through the long years. There were storms; there was revolution; there was war of brother against brother; there was frustration and agony. But there was always this purpose: a nation under God. There was one frontier and then another. The wilderness yielded to the pride and the venturesomeness of men and women. It was still a nation under God. Rivers became highways; prairies became fertile fields; mountains became thoroughfares; hamlets became cities; scarcity turned into plenty. It was still a nation under God.

From a sermon by Dr. Arnold H. Lowe

WE HAD ONE LIKE THAT

"Looks like a smart dog you've got there," remarked a friend.

"Smart? All I gotta say is, 'Are you comin' or ain't ya?' An' he either comes or he doesn't."

FOR THE FEEBLE BODIED

A Chinese who was attending one of our colleges was writing back to China, telling his friends and relatives about American institutions of various kinds.

He defined an American university as follows: "An American university is a vast athletic association where, however, some studies are maintained for the benefit of the feeble bodies."

Col. Edward Davis

TROUBLES

The best place to put your troubles is in your pocket—the one with a hole in it.

YOUR NAME

The Indians used to give their babies only temporary names. They waited until the boys and girls grew older and had earned some kind of name. Thus, some good girl was named Bluebird, Snowflower, Spring Wind, Sunshine, or something else which showed how people felt about her. Some boys, when they grew old enough to join in the hunt, were named Brown Bear, Running Wolf, Black Eagle, or Thunder Stone.

Suppose boys and girls were left nameless today until they grew at least to junior age and had earned some name for themselves. There are some boys who might be called Helping Hand, Brave Lad, Great Heart, Faithful, or Mouth of Truth. There are girls who might be called Sunny Smile, Blue Flower, or Hope.

There are, however, a few boys and girls who might not have such delightful names. There are some who might have to be called Scowler, Shirk, Unreliable, or Cheat. What would be *your* name? *Sunshine Magazine*

THE CAT

The following essay on cats was turned in by a grade school pupil:

"Cats and people are funny animals. Cats have four paws but only one maw. People have forefathers and only one mother.

"When a cat smells a rat he gets excited—so do people.

"Cats carry tails, and a lot of people carry tales, too.

"All cats have fur coats. Some people have fur coats, and the ones who don't have fur coats say catty things about the ones who have them." *The Royal Neighbor*

DEFINITIONS

Asked to write an essay on water little Tommy, after chewing his pencil for a long time, wrote: "Water is a colorless liquid that turns dark when you wash in it."

FATHER'S ADVICE

Fathers should not get too discouraged if their sons reject their advice. It will not be wasted; years later their sons will offer it to their own offspring.

HARD TO BELIEVE

Seeing ourselves as others see us wouldn't do much good, because most of us wouldn't believe what we saw.

VACATION

A vacation is a short period of recreation, preceded by a period of anticipation and followed by a period of recuperation.

IT COULD BE

A story made the rounds in Europe according to the *U. S. News & World Report,* that when Russia's Nikolai Bulganin went to Yugoslavia he did not have time to have a new suit made in Moscow. So he bought some cloth, just enough to make the suit, and took it to a tailor in Belgrade.

"You have enough cloth," said the tailor in Belgrade, "to make an extra pair of trousers."

"How can you do that?" said the astonished Bulganin. "In Russia this cloth would make me just one coat and one pair of trousers. Will you explain?"

"I am sure," said the tailor, "this bolt of cloth will make you a coat and two pairs of trousers. I cannot explain it—it must be because you are not quite as big a man as you were when you left Moscow."

THE BEST THINGS

The best things are nearest, once Robert Louis Stevenson reminded his friends: The breath in your nostrils, light in your eyes, flowers at your feet, duties at your hand, the path of God just before you. Then do not grasp at the stars, but do life's plain, common work as it comes, certain that daily duties and daily bread are the sweetest things of life.

Sunshine Magazine

THEODORE ROOSEVELT'S TEN REASONS FOR GOING TO CHURCH

1. In this actual world, a churchless community, a community where men have abandoned and scoffed at or ignored their religious needs, is a community on the rapid down-grade.

2. Church work and church attendance mean the cultivation of the habit of feeling some responsibility for others.

3. There are enough holidays for most of us. Sundays differ from other holidays in the fact that there are fifty-two of them every year. Therefore on Sundays, go to church.

4. Yes, I know all the excuses. I know that one can worship the Creator in a grove of trees, or by a running brook, or in a man's own house just as well as in a church. But I also know as a matter of cold fact that the average man does not thus worship.

5. He may not hear a good sermon at church. He will hear a sermon by a good man who, with his good wife, is engaged all the week in making hard lives a little easier.

6. He will listen to and take part in reading some beautiful passages from the Bible. And if he is not familiar with the Bible, he has suffered a loss.

7. He will take part in singing some good hymns.

8. He will meet and nod or speak to good, quiet neighbors.

36

9. He will come away feeling a little more charitably toward all the world, even toward those excessively foolish young men who regard church-going as a soft performance.

10. I advocate a man's joining in church work for the sake of showing his faith by his works."

From a sermon by Dr. Edward L. R. Elson of
The National Presbyterian Church, Washington, D. C.

THIS WOULD DO IT

Always drive as though a police car were following you.

WHY I SHOULD JOIN THE CHURCH

1. The Church is a Divine Institution with Christ as its Head and He has invited me to join. John 10:9.

2. I would not want to live and bring up children in this city if there were no churches. To be consistent I ought to be an active church member.

3. Deep down in my heart I believe in the church and know it is a vital force for good in the world.

4. It is selfish and wrong to enjoy the benefits of the church and refuse it as a member.

5. By staying outside the church I am causing others to stay outside too, and if everyone should follow my example there would be no church.

6. I would be speechless in the presence of God at the judgment if I remain indifferent to His church here. Matthew 22:12.   *Bulletin,* First Presbyterian Church, White
Sulphur Springs, West Virginia

AMBITIOUS YOUTH?

The teacher asked his pupils to write an essay telling what they would do if they had a million dollars.

Every pupil except Willie began writing immediately. Willie sat idle, twiddling his fingers.

The teacher collected the papers, and Willie handed in a blank sheet.

"How is this, Willie?" asked the teacher. "Is this your essay? All the other pupils have written two sheets or more while you have done nothing!"

"Well," replied Willie. "That's what I'd do if I had a million dollars!"

HONEST

Lady: "Are you a good little boy?"

Little Boy: "No, ma'm; I'm the kind of child my mother won't let me play with."

STEWARDSHIP OF TALENTS

"I went and hid my talent," said the man in the Gospel lesson (Matthew 25), and he is not the only one on whose tombstone, in the "Cemetery of Neglect" such words are written. Arthur Brisbane, whose syndicated column we read with relish years ago, once penned these words: "The greatest loss to the human race has not been caused by floods or by fire, not by epidemics which have spread disease over vast areas and with the sickle or death mowed down millions, nor by earthquakes and tropical storms; neither by record-breaking crashes of Wall Street . . . the greatest loss . . . has been in the buried talent of God's people." Is there anything more pathetic than a trained teacher who will not teach in Sunday School, a trained voice which will not sing in the choir, an efficient businessman who will not give to God and Church the benefit of his knowledge, a lawyer who will not serve in Church councils so that his Lord can have the benefit of talent which God gave him. We have in every walk of life, men and women who have been blessed, but refuse to be a blessing.

Will someone tell me the difference, in effect, between the person who neglected the talent God gave him and the one who simply misuses it by not using it? Let us think for a moment of Moses. At the burning bush God appears and tells him to lead His children. Moses is pretty well satisfied with his present lot, and ventured to say that it was a bit hazardous (he was only looking for an excuse not to use his talents). God asked him "What is that in thine hand?" It was a rod. God told him to use it. And we know the story after that. God has given into our hands a talent also, and He expects us to use it. It might not be, in our estimation, a "big" talent at all, but we are to serve where we are with what we have. Here is a poem which is pertinent to the point. It is by Alice Bennett:

"I have no voice for singing, I cannot make a speech,
I have no gift for music, I know I cannot teach.
I am no good at leading, I cannot 'organize,'
And anything I write would never win a prize.
But at roll call at meetings, I always answer 'here.'
When others are performing, I lend a listening ear.
After the program's over, I praise its every part,
My words are not to flatter; I mean it from my heart.
It seems my only talent is neither big nor rare,
Just to listen and encourage and to fill a vacant chair.
But all the gifted people could not so brightly shine,
Were it not for those who use a talent such as mine."

R. R. Belter

FAILURE AND SUCCESS

"Of all my inventions," Thomas A. Edison reminisced, some years before his death on October 18, 1931, "the incandescent light was the most difficult."

One October evening, the thirty-two-year-old inventor sat in his laboratory, weary from thirteen months of repeated failure to find a filament that would stand the stress of electric current. The scientific press, at first politely skeptical, were now openly derisive. Discouraged backers were refusing to put up further funds.

Idly Edison picked up a bit of lampblack mixed with tar, rolled it into a thread—"Thread," he mused, ". . . thread . . .

thread . . . carbonized cotton thread." He had tried every known metal. Now he'd turn to the vegetable kingdom.

It required five hours to carbonize a length of thread in a muffle furnace. The first one broke before it could be removed from the mold; likewise a second and a third. An entire spool of thread was consumed; then a second spool. Finally, a perfect filament emerged, only to be broken in an effort to insert it into the vacuum tube. Another was destroyed when a jeweler's screw driver fell against it. After two days and two nights the filament was successfully inserted. The bulb was exhausted of air and sealed, the current turned on. "The sight we had so long desired to see met our eyes."

And then Edison, after working continuously for forty-eight hours, sat for an additional forty-five hours—until the light blinked out—gazing intently at the world's first incandescent electric lamp. *From Gospel Banner*

THE HEART

If you use the heart with which you reprove others to reprove yourself, there will be fewer faults: if you use the heart with which you forgive yourself to forgive others, there will be perfect friendship. *S. C. Champion*

OPPORTUNITIES

Many grownups do with opportunities as children do at the seashore. They fill their hands with sand, and then let the grains fall through, till they are gone. *Henry F. Henrichs*

A PERFECT DAY

You have not lived a perfect day, even though you have earned your money, unless you have done something for someone who will never be able to repay you. *Ruth Smeltzer*

EXPERIENCE

Experience is not what happens to you; it is what you do
with what happens to you.   *Huxley*

DEEDS

Small deeds done are better than great deeds planned.
                                    Peter Marshall

I FOUND ALL THIS

A room of quiet, a temple of peace;
The home of faith, where doubtings cease.
A house of comfort, where hope is given,
A source of strength to make earth heaven;
A shrine of worship, a place to pray—
I found all this in my church today.
                Anon. in The Cheer-up Sheet

MODERN YOUTH

Bobbie was in a store with his mother, when he was given a
stick of candy by one of the clerks.
"What must you say, Bobbie?"
"Charge it," Bobbie replied.

IF THIS HAPPENED

. If all the sleeping folks will wake up,
And all the lukewarm folks will fire up,
And all the dishonest folks will confess up,
And all the disgruntled folks will sweeten up,
And all the discouraged folks will cheer up,
And all the depressed folks will look up,
And all the estranged folks will make up,

And all the dry bones will shake up,
And all the Christians will stand up
Then you can have the Kingdom on earth.
From the Sunday Bulletin of the
Foundry Church, Washington, D. C.

STEWARDSHIP OF TREASURES

Luke 16:2. Give an Account of Thy Stewardship.

Stewardship is a "touchy" subject, because men seem to resent any mention of money from the pulpit, even though Scripture does discuss it in plain words. It is a provocative subject, and men will always when it is mentioned, inject many pros and cons into the conversation. Strangely enough, "GIVING AN ACCOUNT" of stewardship seems to be the most difficult phase of it. We know how the widow gave when Jesus sat over against the treasury and watched (Mark 12), how Ananias and Sapphira lied about their giving and how they were punished for telling the untruth (Acts 5). We might thrill as we recall Paul's statement to the Corinthians about the Macedonians giving themselves before they gave their gift. We might even feel that we know what our neighbor ought to give to the Church. However, it is another matter when we sit down to take inventory of our own "take home pay." But that is what the text asks us to do. It states: "Give an account of THY stewardship." It means to sit down and strike a trial balance, in the words of an accountant, and to see where we stand.   *R. R. Belter*

CRITICISM

Why is it that men and women grow great and strong and creative under criticism, in suffering, and in sorrow? So often it is through pain and in hardship that God puts a song in the heart, and creative energy in the brain.

Criticism is a form of suffering which most people encounter fairly early in life, and the pain is intensely real and poignant. Most human beings desire social approval. Men and women appreciate approbation. To be accepted, to be popular, is a better way of life than to live under disdain and disapproval. Yet men and women who accomplish most in life sometimes receive the severest criticism. . . .

It is not that we get criticism—nor that it hurts—but rather how we manage criticism which is the measure of our character. . . .

Someone had hard words for Andrew Jackson when they said, "The President is a monster whose choicest ailment is human blood." Yet Jackson gave his critic a cabinet post.

"The President is a low, cunning clown. He is the original gorilla. Those who seek the ape-man are fools to travel all the way to Africa when what they are after can be so readily located in Springfield, Illinois." This critic was speaking of the man whose monument is the most beautiful in this city, Abraham Lincoln.

"He is treacherous in private friendships, a hypocrite in public life, an impostor who has either abandoned all good principles, or else never had any." This was somebody's view of Washington.

All of us suffer in some way or other the criticism of others. How do we use it? Do we ask if it is true and, if true, do we make revision; and if not true, do we give it all back to God for his dealing? Do we remember Jesus who died trying to combine all that was holiest in tradition with all that was healthiest in innovation, who unflinchingly spoke the truth, and who "when accused opened not His mouth"?

Suffering from personal abuse and criticism can be carried in the majesty of human personality and turned into a testimony for God.   *Dr. Edward L. R. Elson*

A GOOD LESSON ANY TIME

Nurse, showing a new patient to his room, "Now," she said, "we want you to be happy and enjoy yourself while here, so if there is anything you want that we haven't got, let me know and I'll show you how to get along without it."

THREE KINDS OF PEOPLE

There are three kinds of people: those who make things happen, those who watch things happen, and those who have no idea what has happened.

JUST SPREADING HAPPINESS

"Well, I did my good deed today. I made at least a hundred people happy."

"How is that?"

"I chased my hat when the wind blew it down the street."

OPTIMIST

After a Junior High School class toured the White House, the teacher asked each student to write impressions of the visit. One boy wrote: "I was especially glad to have this opportunity to visit my future home."

NEXT QUESTION

Little Tommy had spent his first day at school.

"What happened at school today, Tommy?" his mother asked when he returned home.

"Oh, nothin'," said Tommy. "A woman wanted to know how to spell 'cat,' and I told her."

SOMETIMES IT SEEMS THAT WAY

The difference between a human being ten years of age and one fifty years of age lies altogether in the matter of toys.

Austin O'Malley

A LITTLE BOY

Lynn Harold Hough tells of a play which had a long run in Paris and evoked profound analysis and comment. It concerned a man who literally burned his way through life surrendering to the hot demands of many vices. In a strange moment of awareness he seemed to stand at the foot of a wide stairway in his boyhood home. Above him, at the turn of the stairs, stood a little lad with innocent, shining face. Gazing at the happy face, the jaded man cried out bitterly, "Once I was that little boy!"

One of the deepest questions which arises in every age is raised by those who ask, "Is there any way for the man in whose life so much has been burned out to get back to the little boy whose eager expectation reached out for a better life?" . . .

The triumphant Christ is perpetually kindling in human hearts the fire of faith which must glow brightly if we are to be great and good and strong. Christ's fire brings life. His resurrection brings new life and vigor to dead men's hopes.

The heart of our faith is that human life can recover its lost radiance. Man can be born again of the spirit. Human personality may be remodeled, and human character rehabilitated. A man can find again his pristine life when he encounters the living Christ, when he comes to him in contrition, claims his forgiveness by faith, and reclaims the lost lustre of an earlier year.   *Dr. Edward L. R. Elson*

SERMONS AND SUNDAY SCHOOL LESSONS

"I see in your church convention," said an old farmer to a minister, "that you discuss the subject how to get people to attend church. I have never heard a single address at a farmers' convention on how to get the cattle to come to the feed rack. We spend our time discussing the best kind of feed."

A NEW IDEA

Distraught mother, to a group of wild children at a birthday party: "There will be a special prize for the one who goes home first!"

THE MEMORY OF A WRONG

His heart was as great as the world, but there was no room in it to hold the memory of a wrong.

Ralph Waldo Emerson on Abraham Lincoln

MAKING THE MOST OF WHERE YOU ARE

I like trees because they seem more resigned to the way they have to live than other things do. *Willa Cather*

OUR ONLY HOPE

In Charles Lindbergh's recent autobiography he said in part, "To me in youth, science was more important than either man or God. I worshipped science. I realize that to survive one must look beyond the material strength of science. Now I know that when man loses his sense of God he misses the true quality of life. He loses the infinite strength without which no people can survive, the element which war cannot defeat or peace corrupt. Now I understand that spiritual truth is more essential to a nation than the mortar in its cities and walls, for when the actions of a people are unguided by these truths, it is only a matter of time before the walls themselves collapse. The most urgent mission of our time is to understand these truths and to apply them to our way of modern life. It requires a dedication beyond science, beyond self, but the rewards are great, and it is our only hope."

WHOSOEVER SHALL SAY

Whosoever shall say unto this mountain, Be thou removed and be thou cast into the sea; and shall not doubt in his heart, but shall believe that those things which he saith shall come to pass; he shall have whatsoever he saith. Therefore I say unto you, What things soever ye desire, when ye pray, believe that ye receive them, and ye shall receive them.

New Testament: Mark XI, 23, 24

PERPETUAL MOTION

Mealtime is that period of the day when the youngsters sit down to continue their eating.   *Herald, Sparta, Wis.*

FATHER

Father is a fixture, much needed in the home, although he wears no halo above a balding dome. As general fixer-upper he makes a handsome bluff. There's nothing he won't tackle —if pestered long enough.

He loves to give out counsel to daughter and to son, drawn from a former heyday, when things were better done. He may, in his own household, with praise be in arrears, but, young ones, you should hear him brag of you for other ears!

B. L. Bruce in North American Union News

HOW GOD LAID HOLD UPON HIM

Albert Schweitzer, one of the most gifted men of our time, tells us how God laid hold upon him. He went to Africa as a physician "as an act of atonement for the sins the civilized white races of Europe had committed against the primitive black races of Africa." That was his ethical motive. But there was a deeper, a religious motive. He says that as he approached thirty years of age, one insistent thought kept pressing in upon him. He had enjoyed a specially happy youth, he had superbly good health, exceptional power to work, a congenial vocation in which he was both happy and eminent, and he had the prospect of a future with high recognition. Yet this one thought kept coming back to him—"that I must not accept this happiness as a matter of course, but must give something in exchange for it." What could he give in exchange for all his blessings? He pondered and prayed and decided upon this—to go to Africa and "to try and live in the spirit of Jesus." Schweitzer is known to many as an exponent of the philosophy of reverence for all life. But he has lived his own life as a prisoner of the gratitude, the compassion and the sense of responsibility generated in him by Jesus Christ.

Robert Worth Frank

MOTHER'S QUESTION

How does a boy know just how much soap and water to use so that most of the dirt will come off on the towel?

Falcon, Marion County, Ky.

WORTH REMEMBERING

No person was ever honored for what he received. Honor is the reward for what he gave.

He who has truth in his heart need never fear the want of persuasion on his tongue.

There is nothing noble in being superior to some other person. The true nobility is in being superior to your previous self.

LINCOLN

Every man is said to have his peculiar ambition. Whether it be true or not, I can say, for one, that I have no other so great as that of being truly esteemed of my fellow-men, by rendering myself worthy of their esteem. How far I shall succeed in gratifying this ambition is yet to be developed. I am young and unknown to many of you. I was born, and have ever remained, in the most humble walks of life. I have no wealthy or popular relations or friends to recommend me. My case is thrown exclusively upon the independent voters of the country; and, if elected, they will have conferred a favor upon me for which I shall be unremitting in my labors to compensate.

But, if the good people in their wisdom shall see fit to keep me in the background, I have been too familiar with disappointments to be very much chagrined.

Lincoln, to the People of Sangamon, March 9, 1832

VICTORY

In every man's life pilgrimage, however unblest, there are holy places where he is made to feel his kinship with the Divine; where the heavens bend low over his head and angels come and minister unto him. These are the places of sacrifice, the meeting-ground of mortal and immortal, the tents of trial wherein are waged the great spiritual combats of man's life. Here are the tears and agonies and the bloody sweat of Gethsemane. Happy the man who, looking back, can say of himself: "Here, too, was the victory!" *Michael Monahan*

THE BIBLE

You will find the eternal verities in the eternal Book—and only there. The Bible is the record of God's dealings with men, humble men for the most part, men with problems that kept them awake nights, men with doubts that ate into their hearts. The Bible shows what happens when God touches a man, a single individual. *Daniel A. Poling, Courage and Confidence from the Bible*

That book, sir, is the rock on which our republic rests.

Andrew Jackson

In all my perplexities and distresses, the Bible has never failed to give me light and strength. *Robert E. Lee*

So great is my veneration for the Bible that the earlier my children begin to read it the more confident will be my hope that they will prove useful citizens of their country and respectable members of society. I have for many years made it a practice to read through the Bible once every year.

John Quincy Adams

It is impossible to enslave mentally or socially a Bible-reading people. The principles of the Bible are the ground-work of human freedom. *Horace Greeley*

FATHERS AND SONS

One father is more than a hundred schoolmasters.

George Herbert

It is not flesh and blood but the heart which makes us fathers and sons. *Schiller*

The survivorship of a worthy man in his son is a pleasure scarce inferior to the hopes of the continuance of his own life.

Richard Steele

YOU NEVER CAN TELL

The beauty of a Democracy is that you never can tell when a youngster is born what he is going to do with you, and that, no matter how humbly he is born he has got a chance to master the minds and lead the imaginations of the whole country. *Woodrow Wilson*

KINDNESS

'Twas a thief said the last kind word to Christ:
Christ took the kindness, and forgave the theft.

R. Browning

JUDGMENT

The deeds we do, the words we say,
Into still air they seem to fleet,
We count them ever past;

But they shall last,—
In the dread judgment they
And we shall meet.   *John Keble*

HEAVEN

For a cap and bells our lives we pay,
Bubbles we buy with a whole soul's tasking:
'Tis heaven alone that is given away,
'Tis only God may be had for the asking.
                                      J. R. Lowell

THOUGHTS

Medical science advises that hard work will never kill any-one, but there are cases where it scared them half to death.

I believe that the first test of a truly great man is his humility. I do not mean by humility, doubt of his own powers. But really great men have a curious feeling that the greatness is not in them, but through them. And they see something divine in every other man. . . .   *John Ruskin*

We are constantly assured that the churches are empty because preachers insist too much upon doctrine—'dull dogma,' as people call it. The fact is the precise opposite. It is the neglect of dogma that makes for dullness. The Christian faith is the most exciting drama that has ever staggered the imagination of man—and the dogma is the drama.
                                      Dorothy L. Sayers

TIMES CHANGE

"When I was a boy," Grandpa began, "I had to walk seven miles to school, with the snow sometimes up to my neck."

"I had a pretty hard time of it, too," crowed Grandpa's son. "I had to drive a horse and sleigh over four miles of rough dirt road to school. And did my ears freeze."

Then Chester, the 10-year-old grandson, had his turn: "Believe me, I've had some hard times, too. Why one morning last winter we had to ride the whole mile to school in the bus with the heater not working!"

THE HEART OF DEMOCRACY

Primarily democracy is the conviction that there are extraordinary possibilities in ordinary people, and that if we throw wide the doors of opportunity, so that all can bring out the best that is in them, we will get amazing results from unlikely sources, says Dr. Harry Emerson Fosdick.

Shakespeare was the son of a bankrupt butcher and a mother who could not write her name. Beethoven was the son of a consumptive mother, herself the daughter of a cook and drunken father. Schubert was the son of a peasant father, and a mother who had been in domestic service. Faraday, one of the greatest of scientific experimenters of all time, was born over a stable; his father was an invalid blacksmith.

Such facts as these underlie democracy. That is why, with all its discouraging blunders, we must everlastingly believe in it.

Sunshine Magazine

WHAT TIME DOES

Before I married Maggie dear I was her pumpkin pie, her precious peach, her honey lamb, the apple of her eye. But after years of married life this thought I pause to utter; those fancy names are gone, and now I'm just her bread and butter.

The Kalends

KEEPING UP WITH THE JONESES

No wonder it is so hard to save money. The neighbors are always buying things we can't afford.

PRIDE

Oh, why should the spirit of mortal be proud?
Like a swift-fleeting meteor, a fast-flying cloud,
A flash of the lightning, a break of the wave,
He passeth from life to his rest in the grave.

William Knox, Oh, Why . . .
(said to be Lincoln's favorite hymn)

HE THOUGHT IT MADE A DIFFERENCE

Teacher: "If your mother gave you a large apple and a small one, and told you to divide with your brother, which would you give him?"

Johnnie: "Do you mean my little brother or my big brother?"

PRAYER

In prayer the lips ne'er act the winning part
Without the sweet concurrence of the heart.

Herrick

When the last sea is sailed and the last shallow charted,
When the last field is reaped and the last harvest stored,
When the last fire is out and the last guest departed,
Grant the last prayer that I shall pray, Be good to me, O Lord.

Masefield

What things soever ye desire, when ye pray, believe that ye receive them, and ye shall receive them.

New Testament, Mark XI, 24

HARSHNESS OR KINDNESS

You may often be sorry for having said a harsh word. But can you ever remember a time when you regretted having said a kind word?

CH – – CH

Pastors might well place this sign in front of their churches:
This is a Ch – – ch
What is missing?

MONEY

I cannot afford to waste my time making money.
Louis Agassiz, distinguished scientist
(*when offered a large sum for a course of lectures*)

THE INFLUENCE OF THE HOME

A little boy was asked if he knew Jesus. He replied, "No,
but Daddy does; he talks to him over the telephone every day."
It isn't hard to guess what kind of language that child was
hearing in his home.

NOTHING BESIDE REMAINS

I met a traveller from an antique land
Who said: "Two vast and trunkless legs of stone
Stand in the desert. . . .
And on the pedestal these words appear:
'My name is Ozymandias, King of Kings:
Look on my works, ye Mighty, and despair!'
Nothing beside remains. . . ."   *Shelley*

FOREIGNERS

Teacher: "Who was the first man?"
Billy: "George Washington, 'cause he was first in war, first
in peace and first in the hearts of his countrymen."
Teacher: "Wrong answer. Adam was the first man."

Billy: "Oh, well, if you're going to include foreigners, that might be right."

AN OLD CLOCK AND ITS STORY

An old clock in a small store in Linwood, Maryland, is said to bear a strange and impressive inscription as follows:

> Lo! Here I stand by thee in plight,
> To give thee warning day and night.
> For every tick to thee I give
> Cuts short the time thou hast to live.
> Therefore a warning take by me
> To serve thy God, as I serve thee.
> Each day and night be on thy guard,
> And thou shalt have a just reward.

SOMETIMES IT SEEMS THAT WAY

Jackie, a 5 year old, was helping his father clean the trash off the garden. After much pulling and tugging, he pulled up a small cornstalk. "Look, Daddy," he said proudly, "I pulled a big cornstalk all by myself."

"My, my," said the father, "you're a strong boy."

"Yes," said Jackie thoughtfully. "And the whole world was pulling at the other end of it, too!"

THE AGE-OLD CHOICE

The age-old choice comes to every one of us every day of life—"To be ministered unto, or to minister" to others.

PRAYER

When you are too busy to pay the deserved attention to spiritual things, remember the words of Martin Luther: "I have so much to do today that I must spend several hours in prayer."

PROGRESS

Blessed are they who were not satisfied to let well enough alone. All the progress the world has made, we owe to them.

RESENTMENT

"I have waited five years to get even with him, and now I have my chance."

If biography and history teach us anything, it is that great men have almost always refused to poison their spirits with vindictiveness and hate.

Abraham Lincoln amazed the nation by putting into his Cabinet his foremost political enemies. As Secretary of War he chose Stanton, who had characterized him as a clown and a gorilla. He made Seward Secretary of State, knowing that Seward regarded himself as much the abler man. Chase, his Secretary of the Treasury, used his Cabinet influence to promote his own chances for the presidential nomination. It meant nothing to Lincoln so long as Chase kept the confidence of the country and did his work well. When McClellan snubbed him brutally, and Lincoln was urged to replace him, he replied: "I will hold McClellan's horse if only he will give us victories."

Disraeli had the same calm superiority to personal resentment. During his short tenure of power in 1868, he granted a pension to the children of John Leech, the Punch draftsman, who had mercilessly attacked him for thirty years. Now, in 1874, his first action was to offer the highest distinction within his power to Thomas Carlyle, who had formerly asked how much longer John Bull would suffer this absurd monkey to dance on his chest. When a partisan of more vindictive turn expressed his astonishment at his meekness, he replied: "I never trouble to be avenged."

A certain proportion of men feel that they must help balance the scales of justice. They nurse personal injuries; they harbor resentment and accept every opportunity to denounce and criticize. They are never great men. Great men have a calm superiority to resentment.

Great men are too busy.   *Lester Kroepel*

HOW ABOUT $100,000?

The story is told that when Western Union offered to buy the ticker invented by Thomas Edison, the great inventor was unable to name a price. Edison asked for a couple of days to consider it.

Talking the matter over with his wife, she suggested that he ask the company $20,000, but this seemed an exorbitant figure to young Edison.

At the appointed time, Edison returned to the Western Union office, where he was asked if he had decided on a price.

"Why—yes," he hesitated.

"How much?" asked the Western Union official.

Edison tried to say $20,000, but lacked the courage, and just stood there speechless.

The official waited a moment, then broke the silence and said, "Well, how about $100,000?"

WHAT MONEY DOES NOT BRING

Money may be the husk of many things, but not the kernel. It brings you food, but not appetite; medicine, but not health; acquaintance, but not friends; servants, but not loyalty; days of joy, but not peace and happiness.   *Henrik Ibsen*

A HIGHER LOYALTY

Our civilization is apparently not concerned in giving service, but in demanding and getting "rights." Today, man wants what he hasn't earned, reaps what he hasn't sowed. All too common is the philosophy that a man is entitled to anything he can put his hand on. It is the gospel of irresponsibility. It is freedom gone mad. Life needs to be measured in terms of a higher loyalty. The fundamental principle of human society should not be self-will but self-surrender. Without a higher law of service and goodwill, neither democracy nor civilization can survive.   *J. R. Sizoo*

"BEHOLD I STAND AT THE DOOR AND KNOCK: IF ANY MAN HEAR MY VOICE AND OPEN THE DOOR, I WILL COME IN TO HIM"

Christ knocks at the door of the world's bruised and anxious heart. And, He knocks at the door of your heart too. And, you know it, though you may not have recognized it. For three hundred and sixty-four days of the year, you may not understand this Word from St. John's Revelation, but a day comes when suddenly you have found the key and understanding. When life consists of the superficialities of an evening at television, or the theatre, or rooting for our best team on the bleachers, or seeking to find in life's monotony some method by which to "kill time," there is not much chance to hear the gentle knocking of the Lord upon the door of our hearts. *It is in the big silences that we can hear the accent of Galilee.*

For instance, at a funeral service, when you hear the ringing silence, and feel the yawning gulf that separates you from the silence of death that shrouds the casket, and you know in your full heart that once those lips spoke and those eyes were open in sparkling, vital life: *in such sorrow,* if we but listen, we can discern Christ near us, knocking upon the door of our hearts, that we might bid Him come in and share our sorrow, and bear with us our grief.

Or, in the *silence of the night,* when the wide spread of a purple heaven reflects the glittering constellations, and gazing up at the immensities of space, we become conscious of our own insignificance, and the shortness of even the longest human span of life. That, too, was Christ knocking at the door of your heart.

Or, in the *silence of shame,* when we expected the whole universe to crumble around us in judgment, not only for what we had done and done again, but for what we were, and seemed unable to be anything else—the heart in its remorse for sin may hear His gentle knocking.

Or on that day *when you looked through the glass window of the hospital ward,* and saw the strange, little creature surrounded it seemed by an enormous pillow, and, still, still as a rose, and just as bonny; and you knew however unworthy and contemptible you are, this gift from the mystery of the universe was God's gift to both you and your loved one—that, too, was Christ.

And, *in the morning* when resolves are high, and each day gives to every man the chance to make a new beginning, you felt suddenly strong and conquering, and went out into the world again to "knock it for a homer"; and, you believed suddenly in yourself—that, too, was Christ.

"Behold, I stand at the door and knock."

George M. Docherty

WHAT 100,000 CHILDREN VOTED FOR

Dr. R. F. Hertz, a British author and psychologist, has been engaged on a research project of great and wide interest. He has asked almost 100,000 children, between the ages of 8 and 14 and from all walks of life in 24 countries, to make a list of ten rules of behavior for parents.

The list might well cause parents to stop, look, and listen. It ought also to interest the preacher, who is preaching often on the home and its opportunities and hazards. Here is the list of what the majority of the children voted for:

1. Do not quarrel in front of your children.
2. Treat all your children with equal affection.
3. Never lie to a child.
4. There must be mutual tolerance between parents.
5. There should be comradeship between parents and children.

6. Treat your children's friends as welcome visitors in the house.
7. Always answer children's questions.
8. Don't blame or punish your child in the presence of children from next door.
9. Concentrate on your child's good points. Do not over-emphasize his failings.
10. Be constant in your affection and your mood.

Halford E. Luccock and Robert E. Luccock
in Pulpit Digest, August 1956

THE WEAK

I swear because . . .

It is a mark of manliness.

It proves I have self-control.

It indicates how clearly my mind operates.

It makes my conversation pleasing to everybody.

It leaves no doubt in anyone's mind as to my breeding, culture, and refinement.

It indicates that I have been well educated.

It enhances my personality among women and children, and in respectable society.

It is my way of honoring God, who said, "Thou shalt not take the name of the Lord thy God in vain."

And—it is a strong way to express a weak mind.

Hy-Y News

THE ANSWER

"Is your mother home?" inquired a visitor of a small boy who was mowing the lawn.

"You don't suppose I'm cutting this grass because it's too long, do you?" replied the boy.

ONE WAY TO HAVE A CONTENTED MIND

For years, Grandpa Tubbs had been stubborn and crabbed. No one in the village could please him. Then, overnight, he changed. Gentleness and optimism twinkled about him. The villagers were amazed. "Grandpa," he was asked, "what caused you to change so suddenly?"

"Well, sir," the old man replied, "I've been striving all my life for a contented mind. It's done no good, so I've just decided to be contented without it."

THE FIRE OF OUR FAITH

D. L. Moody once recounted a call which he made on a leading citizen in Chicago to persuade him to accept Christ. It was winter, and the two men were seated before an open fireplace, when Moody's host made the assertion that he "could be just as good a Christian outside the church as in it." Moody said nothing but stepped to the fireplace, took the tongs, picked a blazing coal from the fire and set it off by itself. In silence the two watched it smolder and slowly go out. "I see," said the host.

If we neglect worship and attempt to live our lives alone or in a vacuum, the fire of our faith is soon extinguished.

From a sermon by Dr. Edward L. R. Elson
of The National Presbyterian Church, Washington, D. C.

AMERICAN GOODNESS

About 100 years ago, Alexis de Tocqueville, French politician and writer, visited America, and wrote a book about the people he learned to know so well. Among other things, he said this:

"I sought for the greatness and genius of America in her commodious harbors and her ample rivers, and it was not there; in her fertile fields and boundless prairies, and it was not there; in her rich mines and her vast world commerce, and it was not there. Not until I went to the churches of America and heard her pulpits aflame with righteousness did I understand the secret of her genius and power. America is great because she is good, and if America ever ceases to be good, America will cease to be great."

SPEECHES

Scheduled to make an after-dinner speech, a Detroit man became so nervous during the meal that he slipped out and went home.

What this country needs is more speakers like that.

DEFINITION

A mother is a person who, seeing there are only four pieces of pie for five people, promptly announces she never did care for pie.

BLAMING OTHERS

Man is inclined, when in the wrong, to lay the blame on someone else. He is like the small boy who was standing on the cat's tail. The mother, hearing the terrible outburst, called from an adjoining room, "Tommie, stop pulling that cat's tail!" Tommie yelled back, "I'm not pulling the cat's tail; I'm only standing on it. He's the one that's doing the pulling."

STARVATION DIET

A fourth grader was experiencing his first summer away from home at camp.

It was no time at all before his mother received his first brief but poignant letter.

"Dear Mom," it began, "please send me lots of food. All we get here is breakfast, lunch and dinner. Love, Edward."

NOT WORTH THE CANDLE

Many years ago, when candles were the usual means of lighting, if a family wished to play any kind of game in the evening, it cost the price of one candle. Out of this grew the saying which has come down to this day: "The game is not worth the candle."

And thereby comes a lesson. Life has many responsibilities, and makes heavy demands. Many people feel depressed and cynical. For them life is not worth the candle. They turn to many so-called remedies—drinking, gambling, seeking easy money—to escape responsibility, to find relief, or in a mad rush after pleasure to find a dream world. Always they find themselves disappointed.

But there is another way. It is the way of purposeful living and unselfish service. This brings into life the consciousness of a Divine Presence, and the discovery of what it means to live the "more abundant life."   *From Calgary Messenger*

EASTER

The joyous message of the Resurrection speaks also of the defeat of death. For in the Easter dawn, the disciples had seen One coming back out of the shadows to tell them that all was well. What was there left to be afraid of? If at one point in the history of the world the grip of death had been broken, then the myth of death's invincibility is shattered forever. Jesus Christ is "the firstborn of them that slept." Lift up your hearts, be surprised by joy—the joy that comes from the Resurrection of Jesus Christ! From that first Easter the disciples were men aflame with a message which insisted that though men be enslaved by fierce passion, defeated, battered, and disillusioned, the same power that raised Christ from the dead is available, not only at journey's end to save in the hour of death, but available here and now to help men and women live.

In John Masefield's drama, THE TRIAL OF JESUS, there

is a striking passage in which Longinus, the Roman centurion in command of the soldiers at the cross, comes back to Pilate to hand in his report of the day's work. The report is given; then Procula, Pilate's wife, beckons to the centurion and begs him to tell how the Prisoner died. And when the story has been told, "Do you think He is dead?" she suddenly asks. "No, lady," answers Longinus, "I don't." "Then where is He?" "Let loose in the world, lady, where . . . no one can—stop His truth."

After two thousand years we stand again by an empty tomb and, like the disciples, we are surprised by joy. The joy of knowing that life can be lived in abundance and in peace through the power that is given unto us by the risen Christ.

Robert J. Lamont

A CHANCE

My country owes me nothing. It gave me, as it gives every boy and girl, a chance. It gave me schooling, independence of action, opportunity for service, and honor. In no other land could a boy from a country village, without inheritance or influential friends, look forward with unbounded hope.

Herbert Hoover

LORD, REMEMBER ME

Some years ago, Dr. Walter Maier reported that a new play opened in one of Moscow's leading theaters—a blasphemous comedy entitled "CHRIST IN TUXEDO." A packed house saw the first act with a scene featuring a church altar arrayed like a saloon bar with bottles of beer, wine and vodka. Fat priests sat around the altar, raising their arms in drunken toasts. Nuns squatted on the sanctuary floor playing cards. It was another of those degrading exhibitions of atheism which repeatedly marked the Red rebellion against the Saviour and which, despite frequent and increasing attempts to whitewash this horror, should make every American Christian pray and

64

work with redoubled force that such ruinous Godlessness may not overtake our beloved country.

The second act featured Comrade Alexander Rostovsev, a Moscow matinee idol, a dyed-in-the-wool disciple of Marx and a sneering enemy of Jesus. You can imagine, then, how the audience roared, when Rostovsev walked out on the stage impersonating Christ, dressed in a flowing oriental robe and carrying a large New Testament. Soon after his entrance he was to read two verses from the Sermon on the Mount, remove his Palestine gown, and cry out, "Give me my tuxedo and top hat!" Rostovsev, as directed by the script, began to intone slowly: "Blessed are the poor in spirit, for theirs is the kingdom of God. Blessed are they that mourn, for they shall be comforted." Then instead of following his cues and putting on the tuxedo, he stopped as though paralyzed. An uneasy silence gripped the spectators when the smooth, suave actor, his whole body shaking, started to read again: "Blessed are the meek, for they shall inherit the earth. Blessed are they who hunger and thirst after righteousness, for they shall be filled. Blessed are the merciful, for they shall obtain mercy." He finished the forty-one remaining verses of Matthew's fifth chapter before a stunned audience. Backstage other actors in the cast, perhaps thinking that he was drunk, coughed, called, and stamped to urge the star of Moscow's stage on with his forgotten blasphemies. But Rostovsev was no longer a blasphemer. Christ's Word had conquered and converted him; for there, before the footlights, he who had reviled the Crucified, now made the sign of the cross in the Russian Orthodox tradition, and cried out in the prayer of the penitent thief, "Lord, remember me when Thou comest into Thy kingdom!" That was too much for the management. The curtain was lowered, someone announced that Comrade Rostovsev had taken ill suddenly; the performance was canceled.

The heavens must have re-echoed with the special praise of angels who rejoice when one sinner is saved! What a dramatic experience of the working of the Holy Spirit! The startling change from blasphemer to believer was the work of God's

Spirit—the same enlightening God who took St. Paul, bent on destroying the early Christians, and made him the mightiest apostle of all—the same faith-bestowing God who has called every disciple of Christ from the darkness of sin into the light of our Lord's marvelous mercy—the same gracious God who now appeals to all men to put their trust in Jesus Christ. Once, twelve Christ-centered men brought the world under the judgment of God by the very quality of their lives. They moved out from Jerusalem to Judea, to Samaria, and unto the uttermost parts of the earth. History has not yet written the full story of the accomplishments of God's Holy Spirit through men who were dedicated to Him and to the world for whom Christ died.   *Robert J. Lamont*

ADVANCEMENT

After Calvin Coolidge made known that he did not choose to run again for the Presidency, he was besieged by newspaper reporters for a more elaborate statement. It seems that one member of the fourth estate was more persistent than the others.

"Exactly why don't you want to run for President again, Mr. Coolidge?" he inquired.

"No chance for advancement," was the President's reply.

MOTHER

My mother! when I learn'd that thou wast dead,
Say, wast thou conscious of the tears I shed?
Hover'd thy spirit o'er thy sorrowing son,
Wretch even then, life's journey just begun?
Perhaps thou gav'st me, though unseen, a kiss;
Perhaps a tear, if souls can weep in bliss—
Ah, that maternal smile! it answers—Yes.   *Cowper*

Mother is the name for God in the lips and hearts of little children.   *Thackeray*

Who ran to help me when I fell,
And would some pretty story tell,
Or kiss the place to make it well?
My Mother.   *Ann Taylor*

EVERYONE HAS HIS PROBLEM

"Some people hunger for knowledge, some for fame, and some for money," said the Sunday school teacher. "Now, Johnny, what do you hunger for?"

Johnny thought for a moment. Then he said seriously, "I hunger for popcorn."

MISUNDERSTANDING

Half the world's troubles, political, business, and personal, result from misunderstanding. Taking the time to sit down and talk it over has saved nations the security of their people, employers the confidence of their workers, and men the loyalty of friends.   *The Lamp*

DISTURBING ONE'S PEACE OF MIND

The Scripture passages that bother me most are the ones I understand.   *Mark Twain*

IMAGINATION AND HUMOR

Imagination was given to man to compensate him for what he is not; and a sense of humor was provided to console him for what he is.

PATIENCE

The ability to idle your motor when you feel like stripping your gears.

GRUMBLING

"I grumbled because I had to get up early in the morning—until one morning when I couldn't get up."

SECRETS

One of the hardest secrets for a man to keep is his good opinion of himself.

POINT OF VIEW

A boy becomes an adult three years before his parents think he does—and about two years after he thinks he does.

Lewis Hershey

HOW TO LIVE

And behold, a certain lawyer stood up to put him to the test, saying, "Teacher, what shall I do to inherit eternal life?"

And Jesus said to him, "What is written in the law? How do you read?"

And he answered, "You shall love the Lord your God with all your heart, and with all your soul, and with all your strength, and with all your mind; and your neighbor as yourself."

And Jesus said to him, "You have answered right; do this, and you shall live." *From St. Luke 10*

MONEY

Money cannot go to Heaven, but it can do something heavenly here on earth.

AN INDIAN PRAYER

Grant that I may not criticize my neighbor until I have walked a mile in his moccasins.

AS HE SAW IT

The schoolteacher was trying to explain the intricacies of subtraction to his young charges. "You have ten fingers," he said to young Jacques. "Suppose you had three less, what would you have?"

Came the prompt reply, "No music lessons."

CRITICISM

An elderly woman was noted in her village for her good nature, and especially for having a good word for everybody. In fact, she guarded her tongue so very carefully when speaking about people that it became slightly irritating to her friends and relatives who loved to gossip.

One day, when someone in the village had been guilty of an especially mean action, all joined in condemning it, save the little woman with the sweet disposition. Her husband said to her, "Do you know, Mary, I believe you would have a good word for old Satan himself!"

"Well," Mary replied, "he's a very *industrious* body."

NO FAITH IN SIGNS

Two fishermen were driving along a highway when they came to a cross road with a "Closed" sign blocking the main road. However, they noticed that fresh tire tracks led around the sign, so they decided to follow the tire tracks, and disregarded the sign.

They had gone some three miles when the road ended at a broken bridge. The only thing they could do was to turn around. And on passing the road block again, they observed this inscription on the reverse side of the sign: "It really was closed, wasn't it?"

YOUTH

Laugh at "puppy love" if you like, but it's the only thing that can reconcile a boy to washing his neck and ears.

In the old days parents worried about bringing up their children. Nowadays their problem is keeping up with them.

TEACH THEM NOW—TO LOVE ONE ANOTHER

Hate thrives best when planted in the hearts of the young. History bears this out. It is a matter of record in the ruthless attacks on creeds and races in foreign countries, and in some instances in our own fair country, that leaders chose youth, and not elders, to be the aggressors in the assault.

But love thrives equally well when planted in the hearts of the young. It is basic to sow the seeds of kindness and cultivate them in this fertile soil.

Adapted from Milwaukee News-Sentinel

IT CAN BE DID

Don't say the thing's impossible.
The chances are you'll rue it;
Because some fool who doesn't know,
Will come along and do it!

MOTHER AND FATHER

Most of the good things in this life come to us in twos and
threes, dozens and hundreds– plenty of roses, stars, sunsets,
rainbows, brothers and sisters, aunts and cousins, acquaintances
and friends—but only *one* Mother and *one* Father in all this
wide, wide world!"

LOOKING AHEAD

While his birthday party was being planned, little Donald
was asked for a list of friends he would like to invite to the
party.

"I want Aunty Mills, Grandpa Smith, Uncle Dick, and
Grandma Jones, and—."

"But wait a minute, Donald. Every one of those you have
mentioned is an older person!" said Mother.

"Well," replied Donald, "they're the only ones that ever seem
to have any money for presents."

THAT'S ALL

Some people are easily entertained. All you have to do is
sit down and listen to them.

WE OFTEN FORGET

We have been the recipients of the choicest bounties of
heaven. We have grown in numbers, wealth, and power as no
other nation has ever grown. But we have forgotten God. We
have forgotten the gracious hand which preserved us in peace
and multiplied and enriched and strengthened us, and we have
vainly imagined, in the deceitfulness of our hearts, that all
these blessings were produced by some superior wisdom and
virtue of our own. Intoxicated with unbroken success, we have
become too self-sufficient to feel the necessity of redeeming and

preserving grace; too proud to pray to the God that made us.
Lincoln

NERVOUSNESS

After Mark Twain made a trip to the Hawaiian Islands in 1866, his friends persuaded him to give a lecture recounting his experiences. In order to encourage him, since it was to be his first lecture, they promised to have friends in the audience, who would laugh at the proper time.

When Twain appeared on the platform, his knees were knocking so violently together that his friends were afraid he wouldn't last long enough to need their services.

But their services were unnecessary for another reason. His opening remark was: "Julius Caesar is dead, Shakespeare is dead, Napoleon is dead, Abraham Lincoln is dead, and I am far from well myself." This made it difficult for him to proceed with the rest of his talk because of the laughter.

AGE MAKES A DIFFERENCE

Teen-age daughter (as the radio ground out the final notes of the latest swing hit): "Did you ever hear anything so wonderful?"

Father: "Only once, when a truck loaded with empty milk cans bumped another truck filled with live ducks."

ANTIQUES

Two kinds of families are likely to have a house full of antique furniture: the kind with money and the kind with children.

A FATHER'S VISION

It was one bleak morning when Daniel Webster was helping his father build a fence on the rocky New Hampshire farm, that he learned his great ambition was to be fulfilled. He was to go to college!

His father said to him, "Son, we intend to wear our old clothes another year. We have put a second mortgage on our farm. I was denied an education for myself, but I am determined that one of my children, anyhow, shall have a chance to be a scholar."

That night Daniel did not go to bed, so excited with joy was he. But neither did his father, in the room below. Old and failing, he was turning his back upon a retired life of ease, but took up his work anew with a prayer of thankfulness that his boy was to have a chance in the world.

It is no wonder, then, that Daniel Webster became one of the most famous men of his day. After he had become great, he humbly said one day, "The finest gentleman I have ever known, and the most heroic soul, was my father."

BEST ADVICE

It was at a gathering of some newly joined officers that the American general, Mark Clark, was asked: "What, sir, was the best advice you've ever had?"

The General pondered for a few moments. "The best advice I ever had," he said at length, "was to marry the girl I did."

"And who, sir, gave you that advice?" asked another young officer.

Snapped General Clark: "She did."

OUR INHERITANCE

Our inheritance of well-founded, slowly conceived codes of honor, morals and manners, the passionate convictions which so many hundreds of millions share together of the principles of freedom and justice, are far more precious to us than anything which science could bestow.   *Winston Churchill*

THE REDBUD TREE

Along the fence rows and footing of the hills, the redbud trees are in bloom, and it is Spring and Eastertime. Once again the redbuds are blushing in shame for their sister tree of long ago. Perhaps you do not know the story. It is a very old one.

From the beginning of time the tree we know as the redbud tree had borne each Spring lovely white blossoms as delicate and sheer as the clouds in the Springtime sky. And everyone who walked along the roadside commented on their beauty, and cut off great branches to carry home. No flower in all the world was more sought after for festive decorations. But one spring there was a tragedy.

A man named Judas Iscariot betrayed his friend to his enemies for a measly sum of money, and his friend was condemned to die. Then Judas, when he saw that he was condemned, repented of his act and brought again the thirty pieces of silver to the chief priests and elders, saying, "I have sinned. I have betrayed innocent blood."

And they laughed at him and said, "What is that to us? You worry about that."

So he cast down the pieces of silver on the floor of the temple and ran away; for he was very desperate, and went out into the woods and hanged himself.

He did not know that it was a warm April day. He did not know that the birds were singing and that everywhere the wild flowers were pushing their heads up toward the sun. Nor did he know that it was beneath the wild branches of the lovely, white blossom tree that he tore his cloak in strips and made it into a rope with which he hanged himself. He only knew that he had no desire to live any longer. It is a great wrong to betray a friend and a great sin to be so greedy for money.

Judas swayed incongruously from the wide branch of the white blossom tree until the people came and found him there. They took him down with unsympathetic hands and were ready to carry his body away when one of them exclaimed,

"See, the white blossom tree has turned red. It could not bear the shame."

And to this day some call it the Judas tree and others the redbud; but no one has called it the white blossom tree since that Springtime long ago.   *By Ethel Crow*

FREEDOM TO WORK

Lawrence Tibbett, internationally famous opera star, first saw the inside of the Metropolitan Opera House from a $2.20 standing room space, because he could not afford to buy a seat.

Andrew Carnegie, the great steel magnate who made millions of dollars in his lifetime, was paid two cents an hour on his first job.

These persons, like thousands of others of our successful business and professional men, started at the bottom, and by their own efforts, and the freedom to work in their own way, became outstanding men.

DOWNTRODDEN

"It's becoming increasingly difficult to reach the downtrodden masses in America," a Communist wrote to his superior. "In the spring they're forever polishing their cars. In the summer they take vacations. In the fall they go to the world series and football games. And in the winter you can't get them away from their television sets. Please give me suggestions on how to let them know how oppressed they are."

800 MILLION PEOPLE

Eleven hundred million people, almost two-thirds of the world, are "voiceless," cannot read or write.

In Asia and Africa, over a billion people are illiterate—over half the human race. This cold print cannot tell you what that means. You may think it is a pity they cannot read, but the real tragedy is that they cannot speak. They are the silent victims, the forgotten men, driven like animals, who have mutely submitted in every age before and since the pyramids were built.

Frank C. Laubach, missionary educator

ABE LINCOLN

Five days before his nomination in 1860, the *Chicago Tribune* printed an editorial profile of Abraham Lincoln. The editorial follows:

Ten thousand inquiries will be made as to the looks, and habits, tastes, and other characteristics of Honest Old Abe. We anticipate a few of them.

Mr. Lincoln stands 6 feet 4 inches high in his stockings. His frame is not muscular, but gaunt and wiry; his arms are long, but not unreasonably so for a person of his height; his lower limbs are not disproportioned to his body. In walking, his gait, though firm, is never brisk. He steps slowly and deliberately, almost always with his head inclined forward and his hands clasped behind his back. In matters of dress he is by no means precise. Always clean, he is never fashionable; he is careless, but not slovenly.

In manner he is remarkably cordial and, at the same time, simple. His politeness is always sincere but never elaborate and oppressive. A warm shake of the hand and a warmer smile of recognition are his methods of greeting his friends. At rest his features, though those of a man of mark, are not such as belong to a handsome man; but when his fine dark gray eyes are lighted up by any emotion, and his features begin their play, he would be chosen from among a crowd as one who had in him not only the kindly sentiments which women love, but the heavier metal of which full-grown men and Presidents are made.

His hair is black, and though thin is wiry. His head sits well on his shoulders, but beyond that it defies description. It nearer resembles that of Clay than that of Webster; but is unlike either. It is very large and phrenologically well proportioned, betokening power in all its developments. A slightly Roman nose, a wide-cut mouth, and a dark complexion, with the appearance of having been weatherbeaten, complete the description.

In his personal habits Mr. Lincoln is as simple as a child. He loves a good dinner and eats with the appetite which goes with a great brain; but his food is plain and nutritious. He never drinks intoxicating liquors of any sort, not even a glass of wine. He is not addicted to tobacco in any of its shapes. He never was accused of a licentious act in all his life. He never uses profane language. A friend says that once, when in towering rage in consequence of the effort of certain parties to perpetrate a fraud on the State, he was heard to say, "They shan't do it, damn 'em!" but beyond an expression of that kind, his bitterest feelings never carry him. He never gambles; we doubt if he ever indulges in any games of chance.

He is particularly cautious about incurring pecuniary obligations for any purpose whatever, and in debt he is never content until the score is discharged. We presume he owes no man a dollar. He never speculates. The rage for the sudden acquisition of wealth never took hold of him. His gains from his profession have been moderate, but sufficient for his purposes. While others have dreamed of gold, he has been in pursuit of knowledge.

In all his dealings he has the reputation of being generous but exact, and, above all, religiously honest. He would be a bold man who would say that Abraham Lincoln ever wronged anyone out of a cent, or even spent a dollar that he had not honestly earned. His struggles in early life have made him careful of money; but his generosity with his own is proverbial.

He is a regular attendant upon religious worship, and though not a communicant, is a pewholder and liberal supporter of the Presbyterian Church in Springfield, to which Mrs. Lincoln belongs.

He is a scrupulous teller of the truth—too exact in his notions to suit the atmosphere of Washington as it now is. His enemies may say that he tells "black Republican lies," but no man ever charged that in a professional capacity, or as a citizen dealing with his neighbors, he would depart from the Scriptures.

At home he lives like a gentleman of modest means and simple tastes. A good-size house of wood, simple but tastefully furnished, surrounded by trees and flowers, is his own, and there he lives at peace with himself, the idol of his family, and for his honesty, ability, and patriotism, the admiration of his countrymen.

A BOY'S PRAYER

Little Frederick was saying his prayers one night. His mother tiptoed up and heard him say: "And please make Tommy stop throwing things at me. You may remember, I've mentioned this before. He's still doing it."

MODERN YOUTH

The Sunday school teacher was describing how Lot's wife looked back and suddenly turned into a pillar of salt.

"My mother looked back once while she was driving," contributed little Johnny, "and she turned into a telephone pole."

AS WE SEE OTHERS

"What funny names these towns in the news have," remarked a man from Schenectady as he read a Poughkeepsie newspaper on his way to meet a friend in Hackensack.

SO SAY WE ALL

An overworked farmer, on being asked what time he got up to go to work, said, "Man, I don't go to work; I wake up right in the middle of it."

WHAT GOOD CAN I DO

Benjamin Franklin was a wise man. He once said, "The noblest question in the world is this: 'What good can I do in it?'"

In working for and with others, we benefit ourselves more than we benefit them. No one is useless in this world who helps someone else. No one can be truly happy who lives and works only for himself.

THINGS YOU NEVER REGRET

Showing kindness to an aged person. Destroying the letter written in anger. Offering the apology that saves a friendship. Stopping a scandal that is wrecking a reputation. Helping a boy find himself. Taking time to show consideration to your parents. Remembering God in all things.

Adapted from Roy L. Smith

IS HE FAIR TO THE UNFAIR?

Because a man is said to be fair and square with those who trust him is not a great recommendation in itself. The important thing is this: Can he rise above those who are unfair to him?

HONEST WORK

Congress can legislate till doomsday, but the economic basis of national prosperity is always an honest day's work.

WHAT THE WORLD NEEDS

The world is not perishing for the want of clever or talented or well-meaning men. It is perishing for the want of men of courage and resolution who, in devotion to the cause of right

and truth, can rise above personal feeling and private ambition.
Robert James McCracken, pastor Riverside Church

SOME MODERN NOVELS

Reading one of the old Victorian novels after wading through some current "best sellers," is like strolling through a sweet old-fashioned garden after a visit to the glue works.

DUTIES OF THE HOME

One of the chief hindrances to decent education in America today is the overloading of our schools by placing on their shoulders responsibilities which in other times and other countries have, as a matter of course, been assumed by the home.
Bernard Iddings Bell, educator and clergyman

CONTENT

When God sorts out the weather and sends rain,
Why rain's my choice.   *James Whitcomb Riley*

REACTIONARY

People who are still driving 1-color cars are secretly tagged by their neighbors as almost as reactionary as people who take care of their own children.

OTHERWISE UNCHANGED

An antique collector, passing through a small village, stopped to watch an old man chopping wood with an ancient ax.

"That's a mighty old ax you have there," remarked the collector.

"Yes," said the villager, "it once belonged to George Washington."

"Not really!" gasped the collector. "It's certainly stood up well."

"Of course," admitted the old man, "it's had three new handles and two new heads."

AS CHILDREN SEE US

Two little girls were playing and one pretended that she wanted to rent the other's playhouse.

"Have you any parents?" asked the owner of the playhouse.

"Yes, two," was the reply.

"I'm sorry," said the tiny landlady, "but I never rent to children with parents. They're so noisy and destructive."

ALL PREPARED

Deborah, six years old, was fully prepared for her father when he returned from work this evening.

"Smile, Daddy," she said, "and keep smiling while I tell you something . . . I broke the screen door this morning."

HUMBLE IMPORTANCE

Christ has the power to make us become important. There is a sense, of course, in which Christianity makes men recognize their limitations and weaknesses. It destroys human pride and exalts God over all. But it does not make men helpless and hopeless, as some modern theology suggests. It gives men a new sense of their legitimate importance and dignity.

This is in the nature of a paradox for, while it makes men most humble, it also makes men most significant. We are the ones for whom Christ died, but we are to be the servants of all. This new status of humble importance is one of the great things Christ helps us to achieve.   *Bishop Gerald Kennedy*

TACT

Little Tommy had just returned from a birthday party and was asked by his mother, "I hope you didn't ask for a second piece of cake."

"No, I only asked Mrs. Smith for the recipe so you could make some like it. She gave me two more pieces."

REFLECTIONS

There are no hopeless situations; there are only men who have grown hopeless about them.

To smile at the jest which plants a thorn in another's breast is to become a principal in the mischief.   *Sheridan*

What lies behind us and what lies before us are tiny matters compared to what lies within us.   *William Morrow*

He who is wrapped up in himself makes a mighty small package.

No man is too big to be kind and courteous, but many men are too little.

FATHER

Joe (greeting friend he hadn't seen for some time): "Well, Jim, who are you working for now?"

Jim: "Same people—a fine wife and three grand youngsters."

A SHARP TONGUE

The sharp tongue of composer Johannes Brahms cost him many a friend among his contemporaries. On one occasion a rival composer of little talent asked him:

"Have you heard my last composition, maestro?"

"I sincerely hope so," was Brahms' rejoinder.

THE CHURCH

The Church can lay valid claim to a scant 50% of our population, but it provides 75% of our home owners, 80% of our college students and approximately 90% of all our support of all good and useful philanthropic enterprises. When it comes to criminal classes the record of the church goes into reverse. The names of only 2% of all American criminals can be found on the records of any church.

Chicago Presbyterian (May 1956)

ALL TIMES ARE GOD'S SEASON

In heaven it is always autumn, his mercies are ever in their maturity. We ask our daily bread, and God never says you should have come yesterday, he never says you must again tomorrow, but today if you will hear his voice, today he will hear you. . . . He brought light out of darkness, not out of a lesser light; he can bring thy summer out of winter, though thou have no spring; though in the ways of fortune, or understanding, or conscience, thou have been benighted till now, wintered and frozen, clouded and eclipsed, damped and numbed, smothered and stupefied till now, now God comes to thee, not as the dawning of the day, not as the bird in spring, but as the sun at noon to illustrate all shadows, as the sheaves in harvest, to fill all penuries, all occasions invite his mercies, and all times are his season.

*John Donne in his sermon at St. Paul's
on Christmas Day in the evening, 1624*

AUTHORITY

A little boy, disputing with his sister on some subject, exclaimed: "It's true, for Uncle Bill says so; and if Uncle Bill says so, it is so, even if it isn't so."

TIMES CHANGE

Dear mother used to sit and sew, while listening to the radio. Our socks were darned, our buttons tight; neatly she mended every night.

Now, two buttons off Dad's shirt I see—for who can sew and watch T.V.?

THE TEST

It's not what you'd do with a million, if riches should e'er be your lot; it's what are you doing at present with the dollar and a quarter you've got?

HE KNEW THE ANSWER

The first grade teacher was supervising the serving of birthday cake and ice cream, brought to school for small Barbara's birthday. As she doled out the treat to one little boy, the teacher looked at his grimy hands and said, "Oh, you'll have to wash those hands first!"

"I don't know why," the little boy replied, "I'm not going to feed it to anybody but me."

FRANKNESS

The music teacher was proudly presenting her pupils in a recital. After a long musical program, ice cream, cake, and fruit were served. One of the young musicians had brought her little brother along as a guest.

As the youngster was taking his departure, the teacher said, "Well, Jim, did you enjoy the recital?"

"I sure did," Jimmie replied happily—"all but the music."

WHEN LIFE BEGINS

When a man wakes up to the fact that his span of life is shortening with every tick of the clock, and if he is going to live a useful life, he must be at it—at that moment life begins for him, no matter what his age. The tragedies of life are with those who drift, and never discover that life has begun. For them the curtain never rises.

THE SUN HAS CONTINUED TO RISE

When George Washington was acting as chairman of the convention that framed our Constitution, he occupied a chair on the back of which was a painting of the sun as it appeared just above the horizon. When, after many months of wrangling and discussions, which often threatened to break up the convention, the Constitution was finally signed by the 39 delegates, Benjamin Franklin, then 83 years old, who had been a great stabilizing force in the convention, rose and said: "I have looked at that painting again and again. I have wondered whether it was a rising or a setting sun, but now I know it is a rising sun."

IDEAS

Ideas are very much like children—our own are very wonderful.

EDUCATION

It's what we learn after we know it all that really counts.

A GOOD CITIZEN LIVING THE GOOD LIFE

As a good citizen earnestly trying to live a good life, you have certain responsibilities if you are to live your best.

For example, if you demand wise and honest government in

your city, your state and your country, you must recognize that wise and honest government is the product of wise and honest citizens, and nothing else.

If you demand that crime be in the cell and not in the saddle, you must support honest law enforcement in your community without any personal privileges or exceptions for yourself.

If you demand unfair advantages, government bonuses, subsidies, and special privileges for your business, your union, your city or your state, remember that the price of class and sectional selfishness is the destruction of a nation's character.

If you demand sound fiscal policies and balanced budgets of your government, you must not advocate expenditures, which, when demanded by all citizens, bring unsound fiscal policies and unbalanced budgets. Every dollar which a government spends comes from the toil and sweat of its citizens.

If you demand freedom of worship for yourself, you must respect the right of other creeds.

If you demand free speech, you must not suppress it in others, or use it to destroy the government from which that privilege flows.

If you demand that a paternalistic government give you complete economic security, you must not forget that a nation's strength comes from each person standing on his own feet.

If you would like to live in a community in which you may have pride, then dedicate yourself in a spirit of humility to your own responsibilities in that community. These are ways in which to live the good life as a citizen.

You may remember the play "Green Pastures." In that play, Noah said to the Lord, "I ain't very much, but I'm all I got."

"I'm all I got." Well, *you* are all *you've* got. The question is "What are *you* going to do with *yourself?*" Will you press for the goal of a great and good life? Will you use yourself to make life richer, better, nobler?

> *From a commencement address at the University of Wisconsin by Herbert V. Prochnow*

RELIEF

Relief! A Texas rancher had some boots made, and they turned out to be too tight. The bootmaker insisted on stretching them.

"Not on your life!" said the rancher. "These boots are gonna stay too tight. Every morning when I get out of bed I got to corral some cows that busted out in the night and mend fences they tore down. All day long I watch my ranch blow away in the dust. After supper I listen to the radio tell about the high price of feed and the low price of beef, and all the time my wife is nagging me to go to the city. Man, when I get ready for bed and pull off these tight boots, that's the only pleasure I get all day!"

ANYWAY, IT'S A REASON

The teacher was trying to impress upon her class the advantages of peace and disarmament. "How many of you object to war?" she asked.

Up went several hands. "Jimmy, tell us why you object to war."

" 'Cause wars make history," replied Jimmy soberly.

PROGRESS

As one old engineer put it: The narrow trails, where two cars could barely pass without colliding, are happily being replaced by six- or eight-lane highways where six or more cars can collide at one time.

A CAREFUL MOTORIST

A motorist is a person who, after seeing a wreck, drives carefully for several blocks.

A DRY LECTURE

Chief-Rain-In-The-Face was persuaded to attend a lecture. When it was all over, someone asked him what he thought of it. "Uh!" he grunted, "big wind, lotta dust, no rain."

PRAYER

As we strive for clear, unbiased judgments and unprejudiced hearts and minds, we might well ponder these wonderful words from a prayer of St. Francis of Assisi:

> Lord, grant that I may seek rather
> To comfort—than to be comforted;
> To understand—than to be understood;
> To love—than to be loved;
> For it is by giving—that one receives;
> It is by self-forgetting—that one finds;
> It is by forgiving—that one is forgiven;
> It is by dying—that one awakens to eternal life.
>
> *First Presbyterian Church Family News,*
> *Evanston, Illinois*

A FAMILIAR CHRISTMAS HYMN

The sound of church bells ringing on Christmas morning gave Charles Wesley, the great Methodist hymnist, the inspiration for one of the most popular Christmas hymns. After serving as organist at the holiday service, he went home and wrote "Hark! the Herald Angels Sing!" a carol that is now sung all over Christendom.

CLASSICAL MUSIC

He was escorting his wife to a concert. They arrived late. "What are they playing?" he whispered to his neighbor.

88

"The Fifth Symphony," replied the man.

"Well, thank goodness," sighed the husband, "I've missed four of them anyway."

FATHERS OF GREAT MEN

The father of Shakespeare was a wool merchant.
The Emperor Diocletian was the son of a slave.
Abraham Lincoln's father was a poor farmer and laborer.
Virgil's father was a porter and for years a slave.
Demosthenes' father, a blacksmith and swordmaker.
Ben Franklin was the son of a soapboiler.
Daniel Webster was the son of a poor farmer.
Christopher Columbus was the son of a weaver.
Sophocles, the Greek poet, was the son of a blacksmith.

TWO LITTLE WORDS

Mr. McTavish's Hotel was losing a lot of towels to guests, even though the towels bore the bright blue imprint, "Ye Ould Scot Inn." The losses stopped completely, however, when McTavish had that imprint preceded by two words: "Stolen from—."

CONFUCIUS NO SAY

Man who leave home to set the world on fire, often come back for more matches.

Little sugar plum today sometimes sour grapes tomorrow.

Man can read some people like book but can't shut them so easily.

Man who beef too much find himself in stew.

Sunshine Magazine

GOOD SENSE

The greatest thing in this world is not so much where we stand, as in what direction we are going.   *Oliver W. Holmes*

There are two ways of being rich. One is to have all you want, the other is to be satisfied with what you have.

No one is useless in this world who lightens the burden of it for someone else.

"Take your needle, my child, and work at your pattern; it will work out a rose by-and-by. Life is like that. One stitch at a time taken patiently, and the pattern will come out all right, like the embroidery."   *Oliver W. Holmes*

GOD'S WILL

When war comes it does no good to say, as men have said for centuries: "God wills it." No war is ever a holy war. War cannot be holy. It is the very antithesis of the will of God. It is the will of God that men shall "beat their swords into plowshares and their spears into pruning hooks." It is the will of God that men should "love one another," even their enemies. Nevertheless with grim and terrible forethought we are preparing weapons of destruction, saying, "We have no king but Caesar." One day, when the holocaust comes we will wonder: "My God why?"

Behind the tragedy will be the same old crowd. There will be the Pharisees, unyielding and proud, saving face and protecting their interests in every corner of the globe. There will be Pilate, washing his hands, and saying: "His blood be upon you and your children," getting out from under and insisting somebody else is altogether to blame. There will be the Master's followers yesterday singing "In the cross of Christ I glory," and today complacently silent, leaving issues to be settled on Caesar's terms. There will be the common people, yesterday welcoming Christ as Saviour and Lord, and then surrendering their minds to the tide and shouting: "We have no king but Caesar."

No war, not even a war against Communism can be a holy war. No war of atomic proportions can be "the will of God" and to assume it as such is to cut the nerve of peaceful effort. Maybe some day we will see that God's will is good will, that love is His way. We can't lose more; we might lose less with the strength of God's will on our side. We have something to give that is better than war planes and tanks. We have a way, "a more excellent way," and a man on a cross who came back from the tomb to lead us aright. His way is God's will; none other will do. *Harold Blake Walker*

MAN

Plainly, this is not an age of meditative man. It is a squinting, sprinting, shoving age. Substitutes for repose are a million-dollar business. Silence, already a nation's most critical shortage, is almost a nasty word. Modern man may or may not be obsolete, but he is certainly wired for sound. *Norman Cousins*

LET GEORGE DO IT

When George W. Goethals went down into the "death zone" of Panama, where 20,000 Frenchmen had perished with yellow fever, most Americans thought digging the canal was so impossible that they began to say, "Let George do it." Here is the origin of the phrase which has been used so many times in shifting responsibility upon others. "Let George do it" has played havoc with human happiness in general. But to Goethals, the obstacle was the biggest opportunity in his life. Not only did he see a completed canal, but he saw a health zone established on each side.

A PRISONER OF CHRIST

I suggest that the deepest thing in the fulfillment of our vocation, the taproot of it all, is a sense of a claim upon us, God's claim, a sense of being a captive, a prisoner of Christ. And may I add this personal word. I do not think I detect in myself any such depth of commitment as I see in Paul and Albert Schweitzer. But there is something in me akin to their commitment, though afar off. I know of no one who has put how I feel so vividly and compactly as George Tyrrell in a letter to Baron Friedrich von Hugel. Tyrrell wrote in the midst of difficult days and amid sharp controversy. This is what he said: "What a relief if one could conscientiously wash one's hands of the whole concern! But then there is that Strange Man upon His Cross who drives one back again and again."

Robert Worth Frank as President of McCormick
Theological Seminary speaking to the students
and faculty of the Seminary

TIMIDITY

A meek little man in a restaurant timidly touched the arm of a man putting on an overcoat. "Excuse me," he said, "but do you happen to be Mr. Smith of Newport?"

"No, I'm not!" the man answered impatiently.

"Oh—er—well," stammered the first man, "you see, I am, and that's his overcoat you're putting on."

SELF-PITY

There is no trace in Christ of self-pity. He suffered the cruelest treatment from his enemies but no word of complaint ever fell from his lips on that account. It would have been understandable if in the last few hours when mounting indignities were heaped upon him—betrayed, deserted, stripped, scourged, spat upon, crucified—he had fallen into self-commiseration. But no! There is no trace, no suggestion of any such thing. There is bewilderment in the cry of dereliction, "My God, my God, why hast Thou forsaken me?" There is agony when he exclaims, "I thirst." But there is no self-pity. On the way to Golgotha, when the cross was on his shoulders and he staggered under its weight, and the great beads of perspiration broke upon his brow, there were women in the crowd who wept. "Daughters of Jerusalem," he said, with simple dignity, "weep not for me." And when they nailed him to the cross and set it up on the summit of the hill, his first thought was not for himself but for others. He prayed for his murderers, "Father, forgive them; they know not what they do." He provided for his mother, "Woman behold thy son; son, behold thy mother." He pardoned the dying thief, "Today shalt thou be with me in Paradise." The self-pitying heart is the self-centered heart. A heart like the heart of Jesus, occupied to the point of obsession with the need of others, is forever secure against self-pity. And the cure for self-pity is there.

Robert J. McCracken

YOU MAY BE A GENIUS

If you think you cannot do much, and that the little you can do is of no value, think on these things:

A shirt waving on a clothesline was the beginning of a great balloon, forerunner of the Zeppelin.

A spider web strung across a garden path was the inspiration for the suspension bridge.

A teakettle singing on the stove suggested the steam engine.

A lantern swinging in a tower gave rise to the pendulum.

An apple falling from a tree was the cause of discovering the law of gravity.   *The War Cry*

BOYS

I remember, I remember
The fir-trees dark and high;
I used to think their slender tops
Were close against the sky:
It was a childish ignorance,
But now 'tis little joy
To know I'm farther off from heav'n
Than when I was a boy.
Thomas Hood, I Remember, I Remember

Across the fields of yesterday
He sometimes comes to me,

A little lad just back from play—
The lad I used to be.

T. S. Jones, Jr., Sometimes

When I was a beggarly boy,
And lived in a cellar damp,
I had not a friend nor a toy,
But I had Aladdin's lamp.

J. R. Lowell, Aladdin

A LONG TIME

A Kansas cyclone hit a farmhouse just before dawn one morning. It lifted the roof off, picked up the beds on which the farmer and his wife slept, and set them down gently in the backyard.

The wife began to cry.

"Don't be scared, Mary," her husband said, "we're not hurt."

Mary continued to cry. "I'm not scared," she responded between the sobs. "I'm just happy, cause this is the first time in fourteen years we've been out together."

LIFE

The little toy dog is covered with dust,
But sturdy and staunch he stands;
And the little toy soldier is red with rust,
And his musket moulds in his hands;
Time was when the little toy dog was new,
And the soldier was passing fair;
And that was the time when our Little Boy Blue
Kissed them and put them there.

Eugene Field, Little Boy Blue

THOUGHTS

Some people think they are worth a lot of money simply because they have it.

Men blame fate for other accidents, but feel personally responsible when they make a hole-in-one.

Medical science advises that hard work will never kill anyone, but there are cases where it scared them half to death.

I believe that the first test of a truly great man is his humility. I do not mean by humility, doubt of his own powers. But really great men have a curious feeling that the greatness is not in them, but through them. And they see something divine in every other man. . . .   *John Ruskin*

ONE THING TO BE SAID

You can say one thing for ignorance—it certainly causes a lot of interesting arguments.

SECURITY

Jesus scandalized the respectable people of his time by eating with "publicans and sinners" and treating them like friends. He even went so far as to call Matthew, a publican, to be one of his disciples. That was like adding insult to injury. Publicans were notoriously dishonest. Zacchaeus, who also was a publican, admitted quite frankly that he had feathered his nest by extortion, but when he became a Christian he returned his ill-gotten gains with interest. Apparently Matthew had been more honest than Zacchaeus. At least there is no evidence to indicate that he had grown rich at his occupation. He was in comfortable circumstances, however . . . When Jesus saw Matthew "sitting at the receipt of custom," he said unto him, "Follow me," and "he arose and followed him." . . .

When Jesus called him, Matthew had to make an important and difficult choice, a choice between economic security and commitment to Christ. He chose the latter. It was a dooms-day choice for Matthew, because the whole of his future hinged upon it. It is an illustration of what Emerson meant when he said that "every day is doom's day," because the choices we make every day determine our destiny. Matthew's choice was not an easy one; not nearly so easy as the brief record suggests. It never is easy to risk security for principle or comfort for loyalty to Christ.

We all want to be secure, free from want and free from fear. Within certain limits security is a legitimate aspiration. To be secure means to be safe, assured, certain, "guarded from danger." . . . We are increasingly security minded, and social security has become a contemporary passion. We want to be secure from the cradle to the grave. You want to be secure and I want to be secure.

What troubles me is the fact that we are making security into an absolute before which all other values make obeisance. All manner of crimes are committed and justified in the name of security. Wars are fought and strikes are called in the name of security. Perjury and murder are committed in the name of security. Atom bombs and hydrogen bombs are created and justified in the name of security. . . .

Love and truth, the absolutes of God, have become altogether relative to security.

When Matthew deserted the "receipt of custom" to follow Jesus, he made a vital judgment of values. While he was a publican, truth and love were sacrificed on the altar of security. When he became a follower of Jesus, security surrendered its right to rule his life. He offered his life to a new absolute to which he gave uncompromising allegiance. Henceforth, security became secondary, truth and love primary. He put first things first and ceased giving first-rate powers to a second-rate project. His whole life was changed.   *Harold B. Walker*

EVERYDAY PHILOSOPHY

You have to save a lot of money if you're going to be comfortable when you die and leave it.

A good neighbor is one who smiles at you over the back fence but doesn't want to borrow anything.

Sometimes a man looks back longingly to the good old days when he had nothing.

Some parents are so busy giving good advice to their children that they fail to set a good example for them.

Knowledge is merely man's ignorance methodically arranged.

There is no man really brilliant who does not know he is ignorant.

If a man has to stand on his dignity, he is very short.

A parent is an optimist who believes Johnny will sound like Beethoven when he plays in a piano recital.

A married couple can live a long and happy life if one of them is unselfish and unspoiled.

Why is it that Spring fever makes a man put his feet on the desk and rest, but it makes a woman clean house and move everything?

It must be hard work for a traffic policeman to stay mad all the time.

Walking is the best exercise in the world, if you can find any place to do it.

The blessing in having twins is that when one cries you can't hear the other.

A road hog is a person who speeds up every time you speed up to get in front of him.

The little boy prayed that he might be made a good boy— but not until the day after tomorrow.

If we could see ourselves as others see us, we would never speak to ourselves again.

DEATH

. . . any man's *death* diminishes *me,* because I am involved in *Mankinde;* and therefore never send to know for whom the *bell* tolls; It tolls for *thee.*   *John Donne*

A FABLE ON LIFE

One night in ancient times three horsemen were riding in a desert. As they crossed the dry bed of the river, out of the darkness a voice called, "Halt!" They obeyed. Then the voice said, "Dismount, and fill your pouches with pebbles."

The three horsemen did as they were told.

Then the voice said, "Remount. You have done well. Tomorrow as the sun rises you will be both glad and sad."

The horsemen rode on, thinking all the while how anyone could be both glad and sad at the same time. As they rode along, the sun became hotter, and the horsemen found the pouches of pebbles heavy and burdensome. They concluded that a few pebbles would suffice for the command of the voice in the desert, and so they lightened their burden by throwing away many of the pebbles, until only a few pebbles remained in each of the pouches.

When the sun rose the next morning, the horsemen reached into their pouches and found that a miracle had happened. The pebbles that remained had been transformed into diamonds, rubies, and other precious stones. It made them very glad to find these riches, and when they remembered the many pebbles they had thrown away, they were very sad.

Sunshine Magazine

THOUGHTS ON VARIOUS SUBJECTS

God has two dwellings: one in heaven, and
the other in a meek and thankful heart.   *Izaak Walton*

We judge ourselves by what we are capable of doing; others judge us by what we have done.   *Longfellow*

Too many people are thinking of security instead of opportunity; they seem more afraid of life than of death.

James F. Byrnes

You cannot control the length of your life, but you can control its breadth, depth, and height.

There is only one person with whom you can profitably compare yourself, and this person is yourself yesterday.

A ship in harbor is safe, but that is not what ships are built for.   *Shedd*

POTATOES AND EDUCATION

"Goodness, Sarah, what a kitchen!" exclaimed Mrs. Hines. "Every pot, pan, and dish is dirty. The table is a perfect litter, and it will take all night to clear things up. What have you been doing?"

"Nothing much, mum," explained Sarah. "Your daughter has just been showing me how they boiled a potato in her Home Economics class."

THE PURPOSE OF THE CHURCH

What are the principal purposes of the Church? These have been expressed in many ways, but certainly everyone will agree that the Church exists: 1. To win men to Christ; 2. To nurture them in grace and truth within the Church; and 3. Through the Church as a beloved community of disciplined believers, to make a redemptive impact upon the contemporary order.

Edward L. R. Elson

AS JUDAS MIGHT HAVE TOLD IT

The soldiers led the way, their torches lighting the Garden and casting weird shadows all about. Then I saw Jesus. He advanced to meet us unafraid. Peter and John were at his side. "Whom seek ye?" he asked as I strode forward and placed a dreadful kiss upon his cheek. The chief priest spoke in a brazen voice, "We seek Jesus of Nazareth." "I am he," the Master answered without a trace of fear. "Take him," the priest commanded. But Peter, my courageous friend, drew his sword as if to fight alone. Hope flamed in my soul for a moment and then it was crushed. The old familiar spirit which I had known so long put an end to all my dreams. The Master spoke again, "Put up thy sword into they sheath, Simon Peter. Shall I not drink of the cup my Father hath given me?"

Sick of heart I turned and fled out into the night. I wandered through the darkness, fell upon my knees, and prayed until my soul began to see. I heard his soft spoken words anew, "This new commandment give I unto you, that ye love one another, even as I have loved you." He loved me, that I know. When my heart was black with traitorous plans, he washed my feet. When he knew I would betray him, he bade me sit beside him at the feast. When he saw that I would go, he gave no sign to save himself, but let me go in peace.

When I returned from praying in the night, I sought again the priests. I took them back their silver bribe and begged them to let him go. But they laughed and mocked me until I hurled their filthy coins upon the floor and fled again into the night.

What can I do? How can I face the world again with my false betrayal upon my heavy heart? Thinkest thou that Jesus would forgive me? Yes, I am sure he would, but oh, my God, I can't forgive myself.   *Harold Blake Walker*

NATIONS AND INDIVIDUALS

The true greatness of nations is in those qualities which constitute the greatness of the individual.   *Charles Sumner*

AM I A CHRISTIAN?

The word "Christian" was first employed in the city of Antioch. A tiny company of the disciples of Christ, fugitives from the persecution that had broken out in Jerusalem, settled there and before long the inhabitants, hearing them speak much of their Master, fell into the habit of designating them by his name. They called them Christians just as in the political world they called the followers of Herod "Herodians" and in the philosophical world the followers of Aristotle "Aristotelians." Actually they fastened on the very factor that bound that tiny company together in a vital unity and fellowship—a personal relation to a living person. That is what is involved in being a Christian. Put at its simplest a Christian is a follower of Christ. He is Christ's servant, pledged to do his will, committed to advance his cause, sworn to loyalty to his person. Who among us will say that in this high sense of the word America is a Christian country? It were better, having discussed it at length, to turn from the wider issue to the personal one. It were better for each one of us, getting right down to fundamentals, to ask: Am I in this high sense of the word a Christian? And if not, why not?   *Robert J. McCracken*

THE SECOND "HALT"

Just how difficult it is to write the simplest instructions, and have their intent understood, is illustrated by this story from *The Wall Street Journal:*

A recruit was having his first session of guard duty. The commanding officer of the post appeared. The rookie halted him. The C.O. had gone only a few paces when the sentry halted him again.

"What's the idea?" the officer demanded. "I just did identify myself."

"I've got my orders," replied the guard stubbornly. "I am supposed to holler 'Halt!' three times and then shoot. You're on your second 'halt' now!"

WE SEE THE BETTER BUT DO THE WORSE

Have we not heard it said that happiness cannot be measured in dollars and cents? We have even said it ourselves. Have we acted as if it were true? Not always. Likewise, we have heard it said that the greatest of all goods are those which can be shared with others without loss to their possessor. A well-furnished mind, a lively appreciation of beauty, a marked capacity for friendship, a noble and kindling devotion—here are goods which, if you have them, I may share. Moreover, if you do share them with me, you will not yourself have less of them. On the contrary, you will have more of them. Do we believe this? In our moments of clearest insight we undoubtedly do. Yet, recognizing the profound and important truth of it, we may, nevertheless, spend most of our lives attempting to collect things which cannot be shared with others.

Consider also the prevailing attitude toward power. Deep down in his heart, who does not know that the only power worth having is power to create something useful or beautiful, or in some way to help people so that their faces light up with joy and hope; power to contribute at least a little to the welfare and progress of mankind? Who among us does not sometimes see with utter clearness that the power of a Napoleon is, after all, both brutish and brief, whereas the power of a Pasteur is glorious and enduring? Yet today it is Napoleonic power that gifted men most commonly seek after. *Ernest Fremont Tittle*

IN LIFE

All that is necessary for the triumph of evil is that good men do nothing.   *Edmund Burke*

People may doubt what you say, but they will always believe what you do.

Truth has only to change hands a few times to become fiction.

TEACHER

A teacher affects eternity; he can never tell where his influence stops.

Henry Adams, The Education of Henry Adams

PARABLE OF THE VACATIONS

Now it came to pass, as summer drew nigh, that Mr. Christian lifted his eyes unto the hills and said: "Lo, the hot days cometh and even now are at hand. Come, let us go into the heights, where cool breezes refresh us and the glorious scenes await."

And Mrs. Christian answered him saying, "Thou speakest wisely, yet there are three or four things that must be done before we go."

"Three things I can think of, but not four," responded **Mr. Christian**. "We must arrange for our flowers to be cared for, our chickens to be fed, and the mail to be forwarded, but the fourth eludes me."

"The fourth is like unto the first three, yet more important than all. Thou shalt dig into thy purse and pay the tithe and give gifts to the work of the Lord, that the Lord's witness may continue to prosper and that it may be well with thee. For verily I say unto thee, thou hast more money now than thou wilt have when thou dost return."

And it came to pass that Mr. Christian paid his tithe for the summer and gave gifts as God had prospered him, and the Lord's messengers and workers rejoiced greatly, saying, "Of a truth, there are those who care for the Lord's work."

And so it was . . .   *The Elim Challenger*

WAR

God how the dead men
Grin by the wall,
Watching the fun
Of the Victory Ball.
Alfred Noyes, A Victory Dance

Another such victory over the Romans, and we are undone.
Pyrrhus

"But what good came of it at last?"
Quoth little Peterkin.
"Why that I cannot tell," said he
"But 't was a famous victory."
Southey, The Battle of Blenheim

PRAYER FOR PEACE

In early December (1955) we held in our Washington Church a Congress of Prayer—attended by many skilled in the art, the talents, and power of prayer, from thirty-six states and many denominations.

On the second day, December 7, which was the anniversary of Pearl Harbor, we received from Japan a thrilling and uplifting message. It began like a letter of St. Paul to an early Christian Church:

"Greetings in the Name of Our Lord Jesus Christ:

It was just 14 years ago today that I led the air raid on Pearl Harbor which precipitated the entry of the United States of America into World War II. But how different it is today, that I am sending a message to a Congress of Prayer, to join in prayer for World Peace.

I am Mitsuo Fuchida, a former Captain in the Japanese Navy, but have since been converted, and am now an earnest witness for Christ . . .

God has turned the message of Pearl Harbor around that I might serve Him in a greater way than I ever have before . . . I believe that the only answer to World Peace is the heavenly peace of God through acceptance of Christ and His forgiveness . . .

With love in our wonderful Lord, I send greetings,
Yours by His Grace,
Mitsuo Fuchida"

Everywhere men are recognizing that one of God's effective instruments for bringing peace is prayer. So, too, in America we are making this discovery.   *Edward L. R. Elson*

FREEDOM AND DUTY

Most of us in the United States believe strongly in free enterprise. But sometimes we forget that freedom and duty always go hand in hand, and that if the free do not accept social responsibility, they will not remain free.   *John Foster Dulles*

A MESSAGE TO YOUNG PEOPLE

Once Thomas Edison was called upon to send a message to a young people's gathering, and this is the message he sent:
"Always be interested in whatever you undertake, or may be

doing for the moment. Dismiss from your minds everything else but the one thing you are doing at the time, and think only of that thing in all its bearings and master it. Don't mind the clock, but keep at it, and let nature indicate the necessity of rest. After resting, go at the work again with the same interest. The world pays big prices for the men who know.

"To accomplish things there must first be an idea that the thing is possible; then the watchword must be *try;* and keep on trying with enthusiasm and a thorough belief in your ability to succeed. If you are convinced that a certain thing can be done, never mind what the world says to the contrary; experiment, never give up.

"Forget entirely the word 'disappointment.' Failures, so called, are but finger posts pointing out the right direction to those who are willing to learn.

"So far as I can see, these principles have influenced me in the years that have passed. In addition, I have always believed that hard work and a living general interest in everything that makes for human progress will make men or women more valuable and acceptable to themselves and to the world."

EVIL

Vice is a monster of so frightful mien,
As to be hated needs but to be seen;
Yet seen too oft, familiar with her face,
We, first endure, then pity, then embrace.

Pope, Essay on Man

USE YOUR TALENTS

Use what talents you possess; the woods would be very silent if no birds sang there except those who sang best.

HOPE

George Frederick Watts once painted Hope as a figure of a woman, blindfolded and bent in tragic, forlorn resignation, sitting on top of the world, playing an instrument, all of whose strings are broken, save one. But, hope to the Christian is a little Child, the Ancient of Days, the Eternal God come down to earth bringing victory to His people. *George M. Docherty*

CHRISTMAS—THE BIRTH OF JESUS

The story of Rip Van Winkle is a fairy tale of a lazy farmer, who lived in the Catskill Mountains above the Hudson River, and who was daily scolded by an irate wife until he left her and went into the hills. Upon drinking some magic wine, he fell asleep for twenty years. But, the point of the tale is deeply significant, and it is this—that when he left his wife, George the Third ruled America, and when he returned, the country was a Republic. The significance of the story is that he slept through a revolution, and didn't know it!

It's well to remind ourselves of the revolution this Child has brought about.

This Child cleft time into the age before his birth and in the years afterward. The staunchest atheist dates his letters from the night of stars in which He was born. He changed men's names, so that we now call our names Christian names. . . . Womanhood took on a new dignity and significance. He not only is an event in history, but His birth made history itself a meaningful event. He founded a civilization that we've almost taken for granted under the name of "western culture." . . .

This Child brought not only new life and revolution to the world, He brought hope, as every child does. . . .

George M. Docherty

THE SPEECHES COME NEXT

The toastmaster at a dinner is the man whose duty it is to inform you that the best part of the evening is over.

TRUTH

Servant of God, well done! well hast thou fought
The better fight, who single hast maintain'd
Against revolted multitudes the cause
Of truth.   *Milton, Paradise Lost*

To thine own self be true,
And it must follow, as the night the day,
Thou canst not then be false to any man.
                    Shakespeare, Hamlet

THE REAL TEST

Billie: "Huh! Bet you didn't have a good time at your birthday party yesterday."
Willie: "Bet I did."
Billie: "Then why aren't you sick today?"

THIEF

'Twas a thief said the last kind word to Christ;
Christ took the kindness and forgave the theft.
                    R. Browning, The Ring and the Book

HOW SOON HE DIES

Catch then, oh catch the transient hour;
Improve each moment as it flies!
Life's a short Summer, man a flower;
He dies—alas! how soon he dies.
                    Samuel Johnson, Winter: An Ode

TURN BACKWARD

Backward, turn backward, O Time, in your flight,
Make me a child again just for tonight!
Elizabeth A. Allen, Rock Me to Sleep

GIVING

The best thing to give to your enemy is forgiveness; to an opponent, tolerance; to a friend, your heart; to your child, a good example; to a father, deference; to your mother, conduct that will make her proud of you; to yourself, respect; to all men, charity.   *Arthur James Balfour, British statesman*

CHRISTIAN STEWARDSHIP

WHAT YOU OWE YOUR CHURCH

Your church blesses childhood in the finest Christian nurture in the home and in the church.

Your church guides and inspires youth in making important decisions.

Your church sanctifies marriage and Christian home life.

Your church seeks earnestly to lead people to accept and follow Jesus Christ as Saviour and Lord.

Your church makes possible inspiring services of worship of God in the beauty of holiness.

Your church fosters a fellowship of Christians with its joy and inspiration to wholesome living.

Your church helps make the community, the nation and the world a desirable place for living for all people.

Your church challenges you to serve your fellowman, to invest your life for good.

Your church helps you in your troubles, comforts you in your sorrows and gives full assurance of the future life.

Your church has brought to you, to your family and to millions of others the richest blessings of salvation, character, fellowship and service.

"Christ loved the church and gave himself up for it." Ephesians 5:25.

Many others have loved and given themselves to make your church possible.

HOW TO PAY YOUR DEBT TO YOUR CHURCH

By Christian stewardship of life.

You are more important than anything else you may offer to your church. Your life, your loyalty and your influence advance the church.

You can teach a class in the Sunday church school or serve on a church committee. You can share your musical talent by singing in the choir. You can visit new church members and make friendly calls on those who are sick.

Your time and talents are needed in the church's program of evangelism, worship, education and service.

Your church requires Christian stewardship of your possessions. With inadequate support the church is handicapped in its service.

Your gifts to the church will help your church serve your community. Your gifts will help to send the gospel of Christ to all the world.

With your tithes and offerings your church may increase its blessings to you and to all peoples.

The Union Church News, Lima, Peru

THOUGHTS

The man of the hour is the husband whose wife told him to wait a minute.

Anything which you are determined to get, but which you don't need, has you in its possession.

We need not all think alike, but we should all think.

LEAVING GOD

A teacher had just been appointed to a position abroad. He informed his seven-year-old daughter that she would soon be making her home in America.

That night the child ended her evening prayer thus: "Goodbye, dear God; I'm going to America."

SORROW

Who ne'er his bread in sorrow ate,
Who ne'er the mournful midnight hours
Weeping upon his bed has sate,
He knows you not, ye Heavenly Powers. *Goethe*

THE YEARS

The years like great black oxen tread the world
And God, the herdsman, goads them on behind.
W. B. Yeats, The Countess Cathleen

THE PRINCIPLES OF A GREAT REPUBLIC

There is no other holiday so characteristically American as Thanksgiving Day; none more historically significant, because its origin is too intimately associated with the beginnings of the American tradition.

The first Thanksgiving Day, as every schoolboy knows, was celebrated at Plymouth, Massachusetts, by the Pilgrim Fathers in 1621. History recounts the story briefly: "When provisions and fuel were laid in for the winter, Governor Bradford appointed a day for Thanksgiving." At this time only forty-nine of the original one hundred persons remained—fifty-one had succumbed during the first grim winter.

The fine character and industry and faith of New England's earliest settlers is evidenced by that first harvest. Despite the bitter cold and hardships imposed upon them by a strange and primitive land, they led an orderly existence. By the end of the first summer, seven houses had been built, and more than twenty acres of land had been cleared. Town meetings had been held, a few laws passed, and the history of New England had begun.

The Pilgrim Fathers, however, were not so much concerned with harvests as they were with those "certain inalienable rights" upon which the American republic was subsequently founded. By choice they accepted the uncertainties of life in a new land in order that they might live according to the dictates of their own conscience. Because that first harvest had been good, they set a day apart in gratitude to God.

The practice was often repeated during the first hundred years, throughout the country, although nowhere was it observed with such zeal as in the New England States. In 1784, for the return of peace, the Congress designated a Thanksgiving Day. Five years later, President Washington honored it. By proclamation President Madison appointed such a day in 1815, and since 1863 the Presidents have invariably issued proclamations naming a Thursday in November of each year as Thanksgiving Day.

Today it is observed by all Americans, whatever their condition in life, because the Pilgrim Fathers were the progenitors of religious and civil liberties in America. The student of American history knows that the principles of a great Republic were assured by that first Thanksgiving Day in 1621. *Uplift*

BOAST AND POMP

The boast of heraldry, the pomp of pow'r,
And all that beauty, all that wealth e'er gave,
Await alike the inevitable hour:
The paths of glory lead but to the grave.

Thomas Gray's Elegy
Written in a Country Churchyard

SILENCE

The ability to speak several languages is an asset, but to be able to hold your tongue in one language is priceless.

He has occasional flashes of silence that make his conversation perfectly delightful.   *Sydney Smith speaking critically of the distinguished Lord Macaulay*

HOME

You can no more measure a home by inches, or weigh it by ounces, than you can set up the boundaries of a summer breeze, or calculate the fragrance of a rose. Home is the love which is in it.   *Edward Whiting*

THEY AGREED

The mother said firmly, "If you two boys can't agree and be quiet, I shall take your pie away."

The younger one replied: "But, Mother, we do agree; Bill wants the biggest piece, and so do I."

TROUBLE

One kind of trouble is enough. Some folks take three kinds at once: all they have now, all they have had, and all they ever expect to have.

THE SCENE AT BETHLEHEM

The ever-vivid scene of Bethlehem—a father, a mother, and a child are there. No religion which began like that could ever lose its character. The first unit of human life, the soul, is there, in the newborn personality of the childhood. But the second unit of human life, the family, is just as truly there in the familiar relation of husband and wife, and the sacred, eternal mystery of motherhood. *Phillips Brooks*

WORTH REMEMBERING

No man in the world ever attempted to wrong another without being injured in return—someway, somehow, somewhere.

Doing an injury puts you below your Enemy; Revenging one makes you but even with him; Forgiving it sets you above him.

It is the biggest mistake in the world to think you are working for someone else. Try to realize that someone is paying you for working for yourself.

FAITH AND WORKS

An old Scotsman was operating a small rowboat for transporting passengers across one of the little lakes in Scotland. One day a passenger noticed that he had carved on one oar the word "Faith" and on the other oar the word "Works." Curiosity led him to ask the meaning of this. The old man said, "I will show you." He dropped one oar and plied the other called "Works," and they just went around in circles. Then he dropped that oar and began to ply the one called "Faith," and the little boat went around in circles again—this time the other way around.

After this demonstration, the old man picked up both "Faith" and "Works" and plying both oars together sped swiftly over the water, explaining to his inquiring passenger, "You see, that is the way it is in life as well as in the boat."

Canadian Churchman

HE LEARNS

There's nothing like a wedding to make a fellow learn; at first he thinks she's his'n, but later learns he's her'n.

MY HOPE

By profession I am a soldier and take pride in that fact but I am prouder, infinitely prouder, to be a father. A soldier destroys in order to build; the father only builds, never destroys. The one has the potentialities of death; the other embodies creation and life. And while the hordes of death are mighty, the battalions of life are mightier still. It is my hope that my son when I am gone will remember me not from the battle but in our home repeating with him our simple daily prayer, "Our Father Who Art In Heaven."

General Douglas MacArthur

CHILDREN

Many a boy at sixteen can't believe that some day he will be as dumb as his Dad.

Too many parents expect strict obedience in other people's children.

CHRISTMAS!

There's more, much more to Christmas
Than candle-light and cheer;
It's the spirit of sweet friendship,
That brightens all the year;
It's thoughtfulness and kindness,
It's hope reborn again,
For peace, for understanding
And for goodwill to men!   *The Churchman*

VIRTUE

I cannot praise a fugitive and cloistered virtue, unexercised and unbreathed, that never sallies out and seeks her adversary, but slinks out of the race where that immortal garland is to be run for, not without dust and heat.   *Milton, Areopagitica*

TOMORROW

Remember that tomorrow begins today. Remember, also, tomorrow does not belong to you. Only today is yours.

PETER

Little Johnny has heard much about his little cousin Peter, although he has never seen him. At long last, he was told Peter was coming for a visit, and Johnny was greatly excited.

That's why nobody could understand it when Johnny took one look at his little cousin and burst into tears of disappointment. "I thought," he sobbed, "that Peter was a rabbit!"

IT'S EASY

"How'd you win the new car, Bill?"

"Oh, I just kept buying corn flakes and sending in the box tops till I earned it. Good car, too. Lots of room to sleep in."

"Sleep in?"

"Sure, the house is full of corn flakes."

VANITY

Lo, all our pomp of yesterday
Is one with Nineveh and Tyre!
Kipling, The Recessional

Oh, Vanity of Vanities!
How wayward the decrees of Fate are;
How very weak the very wise,
How very small the very great are!
Thackeray, Vanitas Vanitatum

HUMILITY AND STRENGTH

Humility leads to strength. It is the highest form of self-respect to admit mistakes, and make amends for them.

THAT'S DIFFERENT

The mother of a little nine-year-old son was strenuously opposed to those murderous television programs that come on so conveniently after school lets out in the afternoon. One early evening, to prove her point, she counted eleven shots heard from the TV set as she was preparing dinner in the kitchen. She immediately ordered the set turned off, exclaiming: "Imagine. A children's program and eleven killings."

Later she heard her little son complaining to his older sister.

"Mother thinks that every time she hears a shot, somebody gets killed. If she'd watch just once, she'd know that they don't do any such thing. There's lots of times they miss."

WORDS WITHOUT MEANING

A little newsboy, too young to read, was weeping on a corner. He was carrying an armload of papers to sell, but was selling none. When a kindly gentleman paused to ask the trouble, the boy held up a paper: "Please, Mister, read me these headlines. I forgot what I am to holler."

IT TAKES EFFORT

No one ever climbed a hill by looking at it.

You can't plow a field by merely turning it over in your mind.

No matter how tall grandpa was, you have to do your own growing.

DON'T BLAME LIFE

One man gets nothing but discord out of a musical instrument; another gets the sweetest harmony. No one claims the instrument is at fault. Life is about like that. The discord is there and the harmony is there. Study to play it correctly, and it will give forth the beauty; play it falsely, and it will give forth the ugliness. Life is not at fault. *Threads*

STANDING ALONE

It is human to stand with the crowd; it is divine to stand alone. It is manlike to follow the people, to drift with the tide; it is God-like to follow a principle, to stem the tide. It is natural to compromise conscience, and follow the social fashion for the sake of gain or pleasure; it is divine to sacrifice both on the altar of truth and duty.

The battle-scarred apostle, in describing his appearance before Nero to answer with his life for believing and teaching contrary to the Roman world, wrote, "No man stood with me, but all men forsook me." But he stood divine.

WE NEED A CLOSER VIEW TO UNDERSTAND

A big-league umpire once remarked that he could never understand how crowds in the grandstand, hundreds of feet from the plate, could see better and judge more accurately than he, when he was never more than seven feet away.

Another man commented that in life, too, we call strikes on a chap when we are too far away to understand. Perhaps, if we had a closer view of the man and his problems, we would reverse our decisions.

LITTLE THINGS COUNT

A thing cannot be too small to deserve attention.

The art of printing was suggested by a man cutting letters in the bark of a tree.

The telescope was the outcome of a boy's amusement with two glasses in his father's shop.

Charles Goodyear neglected his skillet until it was red hot, and this guided him to the manufacture of vulcanized rubber.

The web of a spider suggested to Captain Brown the idea of a suspension bridge.

Watching a spider weave its web gave Robert Bruce the courage to try again.

Henry Ford's idea about a perfect watch plant gave him a plan for his giant motor industry.

EXAMPLE

You can preach a better sermon with your life than with your lips.   *Oliver Goldsmith*

Of all commentaries upon the Scriptures, good examples are the best and the liveliest.   *John Donne*

Few things are harder to put up with than the annoyance of a good example.   *Mark Twain*

THE STOUT HEART

Among the students of one of our well-known colleges some years ago was a young man who was obliged to walk with crutches. He was a stumbling, homely sort of human being, but he was a genius for intelligence, friendliness, and optimism.

During his four years in college, this crippled young man won many scholastic honors. During all this time his friends, out of consideration and respect, refrained from questioning him as to the cause of his deformity. But one day his pal made bold to ask him the fateful question.

"Infantile paralysis," was the brief answer.

"Then tell me," said the friend, "with a misfortune like that, how can you face the world so confidently and without bitterness?"

The young man's eyes smiled, and he tapped his chest with his hand. "Oh," he replied, "you see, it never touched my heart." *The Calumet*

OBSERVATIONS ON LIFE

There is nothing busier than an idle rumor.

Appearances are often deceiving. A woman's thumb may have a man under it.

Face powder may help catch a man, but it's the baking powder that holds him.

HIS AMBITION

When asked what was his greatest ambition, a small boy replied, "I think it is to take Mother away from the dinner table and wash her face."

IF ANY MAN HEAR

The sound of knocking upon a door invariably arouses our immediate interest, and sometimes even fearful curiosity. On the stage, an audience can be held in expectant silence as a heavy hand pounds upon the door upstage. At home, too, especially if we be alone of a winter's evening—outside a high wind howls and hurls cascades of rain against the black window panes, when suddenly in a lull of the wind's moaning, a knock is heard upon the door. At such times our heart can miss a beat. Beethoven, when asked to explain the repetitive, austere, and solitary note at the opening of the first movement of the Fifth Symphony, replied,

"It is Fate knocking at the door."

John, in the Book of Revelation, captures for us this strange unearthly mood of mystery when he sees the Ascended Lord coming again to the world, not upon a white charger, as into battle, nor as a conquering king, lifted high in colorful procession, but, as a solitary figure come out of the darkness of the night to the heart of the sleeping world, and knocking upon its door.

"Behold I stand at the door and knock; if any man hear my voice, and open the door, I will come in to him, and will sup with him, and he with me."

This is the Good News of God. Christ comes to us, and knocking at the door of our heart, patiently awaits our answer. It is as simple as that.   *George M. Docherty*

TOMORROW

Tomorrow I will live, the fool does say;
  Today itself's too late; the wise lived yesterday.
                    Martial (C 66 A.D.) *Epigrams*

  Tomorrow and tomorrow, and tomorrow,
  Creeps in this petty pace from day to day
  To the last syllable of recorded time.
                    William Shakespeare, Macbeth

NOT RESPONSIVE

A young man sauntered leisurely one day into the public library of the city of Chicago. He stood there in the presence of the written record of the accumulated wisdom of the centuries. In that library he could have read the story of man's life and struggles through all history. In that library there were books of history, of science, of religion, of literature, of music, and of art. There were books to enrich the mind and strengthen the life of any person who was willing to make himself responsive to their message.

But this young man was completely unaware of their claim

upon his life. He looked all around, and then asked the clerk at the information desk: "Where are your funny books?"

That young man's unresponsive spirit closed the door to any possible help that might have come to him that day. He lost his chance for growth and enrichment, not because help was unavailable for him; but rather because he himself was not responsive to its presence.

The writer of John's Gospel reminds us that the most tragic aspect of the life and ministry of Jesus was not that he had no help to give, but rather the fact that he offered that help to people and they were not responsive. They were unaware of his claim upon their lives; and they were not the last to stand in his presence and yet lose their chance to have him enrich their lives.   *Leon Russell in Pulpit Digest, August 1956*

THE REAL WASTE OF LIFE

Every year that I live I am more convinced that the waste of life lies in the love we have not given, the powers we have not used, the selfish prudence which will risk nothing, and which, shirking pain, misses happiness as well. *John B. Tabb*

THE BASIS FOR MAN'S UNITY

The contemporary English writer, D. R. Davies observed in his book, "Down Peacock Feathers," of a number of years back: "The supreme irony of the human situation in every age is that the one thing, and the only thing, in which all mankind is concretely at one is sin. And the irrational paradox of it is that it makes any other sort of unity impossible." In other words, our universal tendency to egoistic self-interest, both as individuals and groups, tends to make our differences of background and function occasions for destructive conflict, self-destructive bitterness or both.

The tragedy of human divisions is not in the fact that we differ from each other in so many respects, but rather that our differences become the occasion for destructive feelings, thoughts and actions—and the result is the dilemma of divided man in a divided world. Even when people do get together along lines of common interest, their real although not always admitted purpose is to form an offensive and defensive alliance against those who do not share the same interest. . . .

The various divisions into which mankind separtes itself become the occasions for egoistic self-interest turning both individual life and society at large into an arena rather than a commonwealth. But it is quite another thing to say that the answer to the problem is simply to wipe out the divisions—this is plainly untrue. . . . Divisions of some sort are going to continue to be the experience of mankind, and human sin will not be brought under control simply by suppressing the distinctions between people.

The New Testament, however, sees a different kind of hope for the world. While there will always be divisions between people along all kinds of lines—not only culture, economics and sex, but also special skills, special talents, and special interests, these need not result in destructive conflict. When they are related together to a higher loyalty, these very differences can make possible a richer, more fruitful, more interesting life.

The unity which the New Testament proclaims is this higher loyalty, brought about by the direct influence of Christ in human affairs—in our hearts and in our social life. To the extent that this becomes a reality in the way we look at things, our differences can be seen as complementary rather than primarily as rivalry. And this is precisely what the world needs—a way of meeting the challenges and problems of daily experience on every level, from the family to the nations, not on the basis of egoistic self-interest but in the spirit of a cooperating family.   *Dr. Charles D. Kean*

ACCOUNTABLE TO GOD

Someone asked Daniel Webster: "What is the most solemn thought that has ever entered your mind?" He replied without hesitation: "The most solemn thought I have ever had—and I have it often—is my personal accountability to Almighty God."

We must face the truth that every one of us is accountable to God for the use we make of the blessings that have been entrusted to us.

Fritz Kreisler once said: "I was born with music in my system. It was a gift of God. I did not acquire it. So I did not even deserve thanks for the music. Music is too sacred to be sold. I never look upon the money I earn as my own. It is public money. It is only a fund entrusted to me for proper disbursement . . ."

There it is! Life is too sacred to be bought or sold. The life I have is "only a fund entrusted to me for proper disbursement."   *Leon Russell in Pulpit Digest, August 1956*

PESSIMIST AND OPTIMIST

The extreme of pessimism is that life is not worth living. The extreme of optimism is that everything is for the best in the best of worlds. Neither of these is true.

William Graham Sumner

LIVING EACH DAY IN HIS WILL

I often think of the devotion and consecration demonstrated by missionaries over in Africa. I can never forget my visit to the leper colony at M'Kalama, thousands of miles from here and remote from populated areas and separated from other mission stations because of the dread disease, leprosy. This disease sentences its victims literally to a prison of isolation. As far as their home folks are concerned they are untouchables. What sane person wants dealings with leprosy relatives? There are about four hundred and twenty of them in the particular church hospital I describe. Three young nurses had come from America to minister and work among them. They shared the experience of a recent famine. If you sometimes complain that life gets difficult for you, that its enamel gets chipped, and it isn't as wonderful as it ought to be, stop and think about how some other folks around our world have it.

Well, the famine was so dire that corn had to be rationed. A meager dole of about five gallons of corn a day had to suffice for an entire village. Every single grain was precious. The nurse in telling me the story vividly described these lepers. Their fingers were gone. They had just stubs for hands. They would squat on the ground where the corn was being rationed and try to pick up with these stubs of fists any kernels spilled in the process of measuring. Even these were chewed to appease hunger. She spared none of the gruesome details of the terrific suffering and travail. Then she led me through the hospital to show me some patients. Many had been lepers for as long as eighteen years. You could hardly identify them as human any more. When she told me that she could hardly wait to awaken in the morning in order to get back to work, I interrupted to say: "How can you possibly remain so vibrant and unwearied, surrounded by such suffering?" She answered: "You can't possibly know what a thrill it is to share my life with people who so desperately need help and who also thirstingly yearn for the gospel's message of peace!"

Consider this nurse as typical of that staff. Thrown into this situation far from home, in an environment more tragic than any one of us could dream, she was making a heaven on earth simply by finding in it God's will for her life. She will walk fifteen miles each day along a little path through the jungles, every step of it in danger of unseen and ferocious beasts. Yet she was wholly unafraid. Was it not because she had faith in God, and in believing prayer patiently sought His will and purpose, and then lived each day in His will as it opened up to her? You could tell by the smile on the face of this vibrant girl that she lived the "hidden life" with God, and knew a daily close companionship with her Master. God can bring good to come out of any situation. He makes "all things work together for good," as St. Paul has so aptly put it.

Dr. Reuben Youngdahl in Pulpit Digest, August 1956

CHRIST

There is a green hill far away,
Without a city wall,
Where the dear Lord was crucified,
Who died to save us all.

Cecil Frances Alexander, 1818–95

LOVE

So long as we love, we serve. So long as we are loved by others I would almost say we are indispensable; and no man is useless while he has a friend. *R. L. Stevenson*

WRINKLES

If wrinkles must be written upon our brows, let them not be written upon the heart. The spirit should not grow old.

James A. Garfield

SECRET SORROWS

Believe me, every man has his secret sorrows, which the world knows not; and oftentimes we call a man cold when he is only sad. *Longfellow*

THE CHURCH

A church is God between four walls. *Victor Hugo*

I never weary of great churches. It is my favourite kind of mountain scenery. Mankind was never so happily inspired as when it made a cathedral. *R. L. Stevenson*

I was glad when they said unto me, Let us go into the house of the Lord. *Psalms CXXII, 1*

Where two or three are gathered together in my name, there am I in the midst of them. *Matthew XVIII, 20*

WAR

Give me the money that has been spent in war, and I will clothe every man, woman and child in an attire of which kings and queens would be proud. I will build a schoolhouse in every valley over the whole earth. I will crown every hillside with a place of worship consecrated to the gospel of peace.

Charles Sumner

LOGIC

Two small girls were playing together one afternoon in the park.

"I wonder what time it is," said one of them at last.

"Well, it can't be four o'clock yet," replied the other with magnificent logic, "because my mother said I was to be home at four, and I'm not."

THE CHILD OF GOD

Bad will be the day for every man when he becomes absolutely contented with the life that he is living, with the thoughts that he is thinking, with the deeds that he is doing, when there is not forever beating at the doors of his soul some great desire to do something larger, which he knows that he was meant and made to do because he is still, in spite of all, the child of God.

Phillips Brooks

FRIENDS

Blessed are they who have the gift of making friends, for it is one of God's best gifts. It involves many things, but above all, the power of going out of one's self, and appreciating whatever is noble and loving in another.　　*Thomas Hughes*

YOUR IDEALS

I love you for what you are, but I love you yet more for what you are going to be.

I love you not so much for your realities as for your ideals. I pray for your desires that they may be great, rather than for your satisfactions, which may be so hazardously little.

A satisfied flower is one whose petals are about to fall. The most beautiful rose is one hardly more than a bud wherein the pangs and ecstasies of desire are working for larger and finer growth.

Not always shall you be what you are now.

You are going forward toward something great. I am on the way with you and therefore I love you.   *Carl Sandburg*

TROUBLE STARTS THIS WAY

Charles had obviously been in quite a fight and Mother was trying to ascertain the facts. "Who started it?" she asked.

"Well," replied Charles, "it all began when Sammy hit me back."

CREATION

To me it seems as if when God conceived the world, that was poetry; He formed it, and that was sculpture; He varied and colored it, and that was painting; and then, crowning all, He peopled it with living beings, and that was the grand divine, eternal drama.   *Charlotte Cushman*

GEOGRAPHY

"Is the world round?" the teacher asked the boy.
"No, ma'm."
"Is it flat, then?"
"No, ma'm."

"Are you crazy child? If it isn't round and it isn't flat, what is it?"

"Pop says it's crooked."

BEAUTY

For two decades the life of the great French artist Renoir was one of pain and misery. Rheumatism racked his body and distorted his fingers. Often when he held his brush between thumb and forefinger, and slowly and painfully applied his paints to the canvas, great beads of perspiration broke out upon his brow, because of his suffering.

Renoir could not stand at his work, but had to be placed in a chair, which was moved up and down to give him access to the various parts of his canvas. At intervals a physician administered sedatives, but the suffering was seldom allayed.

Yet the artist nobly persisted, painting in pain his masterpieces, of beauty and enchantment.

"Master," his disciple Matisse pleaded one day, "why do you do more? Why torture yourself?"

Gazing at one of his favorite canvases, Renoir replied, "The pain passes, but the beauty remains."   *Adrian Anderson*

THE RIGHT WAY

President Lincoln was once taken to task for his attitude toward his enemies.

"Why do you try to make friends of them?" asked an associate.

"Am I not destroying my enemies," Lincoln gently replied, "when I make them my friends?"

WE MUST DETERMINE

Sir Wilfred Grenfell, the great English missionary physician, who devoted his life to improving living conditions in Labrador and Newfoundland, would often go to college student bodies for recruits. "We have each to determine," he would say to the students, "whether this world is an arena where we fight to get what we can for ourselves, or a field of honor where we give all we can for our fellow men."

THE DOOR OPENS FROM THE INSIDE

In my study here in Washington, there hangs on the wall above and behind my head a reproduction of Holman Hunt's great picture of Jesus, "Behold I Stand at the Door." Hunt has depicted Christ standing at a door, firmly shut, in the half light of the evening, with His right hand upon the knocker. At His feet, weeds have grown long and rank for the door had not been opened for many a year. Thus, He stands patiently awaiting a response—His head haloed like the corona of a harvest moon, His Kingly Crown entwined with the crown of thorns, in His left hand a lantern, casting a flickering light upon the weeds entwining the door, and showing us the nail-prints in His pierced hands. The picture was presented to me by a lady who requested that it be placed in this position that people who came to visit with me must look upwards towards the Christ we both confess. When the original was first exhibited in London, the critics immediately seized the opportunity to say that Hunt had made one omission. On the door there is a knocker; but there is no outside handle. And, this is true. Hunt had his reply.

"This door opens only from the inside."

For it is the door of man's heart, and it opens only to those who would listen to the voice of the Master.

If any man—not just the good and the pious, and the people of prayer—if any man hear and open the door, Christ will come in.

This is the free offer of the Gospel—without money and without price. Open the door of your heart. Rise up from that chair of ease. Push aside the newspapers and the literature of this world that are filling so much of your life. Take off that coat that stifles your outlook. Break away from the routine of spending your days with your cosy self, comfortable and contented, but woefully confined to the fireside of life. And, by a supreme act of the will, go to the door of your heart, and throw it wide open that Christ might enter.   *George M. Docherty*

CORRECT

Teacher: "Who lived in the Garden of Eden?"
Small Boy: "The Adamses."

TRUTH

He who has truth in his heart need never fear the want of persuasion on his tongue.   *Ruskin*

LOOKING AHEAD

Instead of going to school a boy had gone fishing. On his way home he met one of his school chums. Seeing that the boy was carrying a fishing line, the chum asked, "Catch anything?"

"No," replied the boy, "I haven't been home yet."

SON, TRUTH MAY BE HARD TO HEAR

After his return from church one Sunday a small boy said, "You know what, Mommie? I'm going to be a minister when I grow up."

"That's fine," said his mother. "But what made you decide you want to be a preacher?"

"Well," said the boy pensively, "I'll have to go to church on Sunday anyway, and I think it would be more fun to stand up and yell than to sit still and listen."

HEAVEN

One sweetly solemn thought
Comes to me o'er and o'er;

I am nearer home today
Than I ever have been before.

Phoebe Cary

SUGGESTION BOX

A certain man moved to the country, where he was visited regularly by his city friends. Each one had some suggestion to make for ways he could improve his farm. Finally he put up a "suggestion box" for the "city fellers."

This suggestion box was rather unique in that it was made without a bottom and was hung directly over a wastebasket.

Sunshine Magazine

THE MAN WHO COUNTS

It is not the critic who counts; not the man who points out how the strong man stumbled, or where the doer of a deed could have done better. The credit belongs to the man who . . . strives valiantly, who errs and comes short again and again because there is no effort without error and shortcoming. It is the man who does actually strive to do the deeds, who knows the great enthusiasm, the great devotions, who spends himself in a worthy cause, who at the best knows in the end the triumph of high achievement, and who at the worst, if he fails, at least fails while daring greatly, so that his place shall never be with those cold and timid souls who knew neither victory nor defeat.

Theodore Roosevelt

A FABLE

A frog found himself caught in a very deep rut on a country road, and though his friends tried with might and main to help him get out, their efforts were to no avail. And at last they left him in deepest despair.

The very next day one of these friends was hopping along that country road, and whom did he meet but the same frog who the day before had been hopelessly stuck in the rut of the road.

"Well," the friendly frog said; "I thought you were stuck in that rut for good, and couldn't get out."

"That's right, I couldn't," the first frog said, "but a truck came along—and I *had* to."

Just what would happen if all of us used for even one day the total power of all our resources, which we usually use just when we think we *have* to.

GOOD DEEDS

The only good deeds you can be certain of accomplishing are the ones you do today.

No good deed is so small that it isn't better than the grandest intention.

LIFE

At five: the youngster says: "The stork brought us a new baby sister."

At ten: "My Dad can lick any man twice his size."

At fifteen: "Girls are—blah!"

At twenty: "Just give me a chance, I'll show 'em!"

At twenty-five: "The system is all wrong; I'll show 'em."

At thirty: "I'm going to demand my rights."

At thirty-five: "I'd be rich if I had stayed single."

At forty: "Give me another bottle of vitamins."

At forty-five: "Taxes take everything a man earns."

At fifty-five: "Thank God I've got a good home."

At sixty: "I was mighty lucky to pick such a fine woman."

At sixty-five: "I feel as young as I did twenty years ago."

At seventy: "I don't know what these young people today are coming to."

HEAD OF THE CLASS

"Willie," said teacher, "can you name the principal river of Egypt?"

"It's the Nile, Ma'am."

"That's right. Now can you tell me the names of some of the smaller tributaries?"

Willie hesitated, then smiled. "The juveniles!"

NOT EASY

Here is a list of hard things to do: To apologize, to begin over, to be unselfish, to take advice, to admit error, to be charitable, to keep on trying, to be considerate, to avoid mistakes, to be modest, to profit by mistakes, to think before acting, to forgive and forget, to keep out of the rut, to make the best of little, to look on the bright side of things.

And it always pays!

HARD PROBLEM FOR YOUTH

How can a youngster learn good manners without seeing any?

ONE VIEW

It's a cold, cruel world if you read the front pages: politics, crime, and the cold war rages; the high cost of living, the threat of atomic bombs. You take the front pages—I'll take the comics!

START NOW

Our scientists, inventors, and discoverers have all been men to whom years of hard, persistent labor meant nothing. Consider Harvey who spent eight years discovering the theory of blood circulation. Consider Noah Webster whose dictionary was not regarded a success until after he had worked on it thirty-six years. And consider James Watt who spent twenty years trying to invent a condensing machine.

Robert E. Peary had one great aim in life. That was to discover the North Pole and claim it for America. Seven times he tried, and seven times he failed. But on his eighth venture, when he was fifty-three years old, he discovered it. After twenty-three years of fruitless searching, Peary achieved success. That's how long it took him!

Start on your success path today. Start at the bottom, or as far up the ladder as you can. But start today. Don't expect success tomorrow, nor next week, nor next month. But perhaps you can do it in less time than others have done it. Do you want to try?   *Adapted from The Young Soldier*

IDEAS TO REMEMBER

We might all be more successful if we followed the advice we give others.

It's surprising how much good you can do if you don't care who gets the credit.

THROWING THE FIRST STONE

There is so much good in the worst of us, and so much bad in the best of us, that it's hard to tell which one of us ought to reform the rest of us.

LIFE

We live in deeds, not years; in thoughts, not breaths;
In feelings, not in figures on a dial.
We should count time by heart-throbs.
He most lives
Who thinks most, feels the noblest, acts the best.
                                        Philip James Bailey

OPTIMIST

For a long while the boy had been sitting on the bank of a stream. A man came along and, filled with curiosity, questioned the boy. "How many have you caught?"

"Well," answered the boy without turning around, "if I catch the one I'm after now, then two more, I'll have three."

BUT YOU SHOULD

Little Roger came home from Sunday school with a mite box, which the teacher had given him. "Why do they call it a 'mite box,' Mother?" he asked.

"Because," chirped his little brother before his mother could answer, "because you might put something in it and you might not."

THOUGHTS

Tomorrow is the day that comes before we have worked out today's problems.

When someone says something can't be done, it only means he can't do it.

GRATITUDE

Two kinds of gratitude: the sudden kind
We feel for what we take, the larger kind
We feel for what we give   *E. A. Robinson*

COUNT TEN

Before you flare up at anyone's faults, take time to count ten —ten of your own.

THE GREATEST OF THESE

A Fable

A Persian Ruler once had a wonderful pearl, white and pure and of great price, and this pearl he wished to give to one of his three sons who would show the greatest nobility.

One day he called them to him and said, "During all this past year, what is the greatest deed you have done?"

The oldest son spoke promptly: "When I took my last journey, a merchant gave me some valuable jewels to deliver to safe-keeping. He kept no account of them. I could easily have kept one, or even two, and the merchant would not have missed them. But I gave up the chance of becoming rich, and delivered every one of the jewels to safety."

"You did well, my son, you were honest," said the ruler; "but could you have done differently without having great shame?"

The second son told his story modestly. He said, "I was watching a child play by a lake. Soon he fell in, and I at once plunged in after him and so saved his life."

"You did well, my son, you were brave," said the ruler; "but you could not have left the child to drown."

The third son hesitated. Finally he spoke. "I was coming over the mountain one day, and I saw a man who hates me, and has done me harm. He was asleep and had rolled near the edge of a great precipice. One push would have sent him over. Just passing him by would have left him to move in his sleep and fall to his death. But I waked him gently, and told him of his danger, and he abused me for it."

"My son," declared the ruler, "the pearl is yours. You did right, without the hope of reward, to one who had done you wrong."

INDEX

136

138

142